THE ESSENTIAL GUIDE TO

Jazz Dance

Dollie Henry. SIMON RICHARDSON

THE ESSENTIAL GUIDE TO

Jazz Dance

DOLLIE HENRY AND PAUL JENKINS

THE CROWOOD PRESS

First published in 2019 by
The Crowood Press Ltd
Ramsbury, Marlborough
Wiltshire SN8 2HR

enquiries@crowood.com

www.crowood.com

British Library Cataloguing-in-Publication Data
A catalogue record for this book is available from the British Library.

ISBN 978 1 78500 635 7

All dancers pictured are (or have been) members of BOP Jazz Theatre Company (UK) or are participating dancers in BOP workshops, masterclasses or residencies.

Typeset by Jean Cussons Typesetting, Diss, Norfolk

Printed and bound in India by Parksons Graphics

CONTENTS

PREFACE

For as long as I can remember, the dance, the music and the art form of jazz, has been the conduit through which I have inhabited and embraced my personal and creative life. The jazz art form has always excited me, definitely challenged me, sometimes infuriated me and even frustrated me, but above all it has provided me with a definite purpose and the motivation to pursue my aspirations as a creative dance theatre artist.

When approached to produce a practical guide book for jazz dance, I had a sense of both excitement and panic. To be a jazz practitioner is to share and show the dance through the physical realms, as a dance artist or dance teacher. Jazz is essentially an aural tradition and much of what we do as creative artists is in the 'here and now'. The immediacy and individuality of jazz dance is the very reason that it is often difficult to explain, define and quantify, and yet many of us are intuitively connected to the energy, innovation and creative vibration of jazz expression. Unfortunately, this does not always lend itself to the written page and it is, therefore, not so surprising that there are very few practical or abridged guides to jazz dance. Having just spent the best part of two years working on this book, I can certainly understand why!

To be very clear from the onset, *The Essential Guide to Jazz Dance* and its inherent music is not in any way intended to be an academic tome or, indeed, a re-telling of the entire history of jazz dance. I am not an academic or historian – I am a jazz practitioner, pursuing my creative life through the jazz idiom. Moreover, this jazz book is intended to support students, dancers and dance teachers to place the jazz dance journey and lineage in context, and to communicate the practical and creative elements authenticated by jazz dance innovators of the past, which has led to the development and presentation of the jazz dance form of today.

As with all great art, the creative interpretations and derivatives of jazz dance reach far beyond contextualized and institutionalized understanding. As an art form, jazz dance is unique in that it is traditionally presented as an aural expression, an intuitive and immediate creative expression or, in jazz terms, improvised. The process of the jazz art form is passed on through the shared practice and experience between a community or collective of people – in essence, between the choreographer and dancer, teacher and student, artist/performer and audience.

Therefore, this book is an expression of both my own individual understanding and analysis of the artistic principles, processes, structures and techniques of the important dance practitioners and creators, who have shaped the branches of the jazz dance tree.

The jazz art form is a reflection of real life. Most artists create because they have something to say and to share, be that from a personal, social or cultural point of view. It is, therefore, not surprising that many of us are drawn to express ourselves through the jazz art form.

Over the last forty years, I have been most fortunate in that my performing career and creative experiences have afforded me the opportunities to cross over many times between musical theatre, film and TV, the commercial sector and the artistic dance company setting. Every experience has provided me with the opportunity to grow, learn and draw inspiration from being a jazz choreographer, dance teacher and performing artist.

Immersing myself into the jazz world has enabled me to find a true connection to the root of the genre, the lineage and aesthetic of the jazz idiom. It has also enabled me to find my own truth, style, technique and creative expression as a jazz dance artist and choreographer, which is realized and continues to develop through my jazz theatre company, Body of People (BOP).

Clearly, the language of the body for storytelling is dance. Jazz dance is no different; it is through the individual creative and artistic expression that we see the further development of the jazz dance art form as it moves in rhythm to the creative heartbeat of its practitioners and performers. Personally, I realize that I am innately connected to the pulse of jazz, the dance, the music and all it represents and can represent. The fact is, I did not find jazz, jazz found me.

Dollie Henry
February 2019

INTRODUCTION

There is no mistaking that as a form of art and of entertainment, the jazz idiom originated in America some two centuries ago. Since then, through all its transformations, jazz expression has provided a wealth of creative tributaries to follow that are both artistic and commercial, so making the jazz idiom a truly inclusive art form.

Over the last two hundred plus years, both jazz dance and jazz music have instigated and influenced most of popular entertainment and artistic collaborations. Interestingly, the twists, turns and expressions of jazz music and jazz musicians have long been articulated and, certainly since the days of be-bop, considered artistic high art. This is not always true of jazz dance. There are a multitude of reasons for this, many of which will be discussed later in the book. However, certainly apparent is that jazz dance has, and continues to hold, enormous influence over all other forms of dance, easily identified within its commercial exposure in TV, music, videos, film and, of course, musical theatre and show dance. The jazz voice has also found itself in collaboration with ballet, contemporary dance and is part of the DNA of hip-hop dance and other world dance forms.

There is no denying that jazz influence and effect are still very much alive and kicking. The arms and legs of jazz dance have settled and continue to thrive and strive in many differing countries and cultures in our global dance world. History recalls that through migration, cultural and economic exploitation, politics, social and racial differences, jazz dance has developed, shaped and transformed itself into a unique artistic expression, even though not always recognized for its artistic and creative development in our present dance landscape.

Through its journey, jazz has always created much discussion between critics and audiences, promotors and practitioners, artistes and educationalists; in the early days, it has to be said, not always in a positive light. The American classical choreographer Ruth St. Denis felt that 'jazz dance was vulgar' and clearly John Martin, dance critic of the *New York Times*, was very upset by jazz when, in 1929, he wrote: 'Jazz dance is coarse and its purpose crude; its effect is upon the senses, not upon the emotions or intellect. Such is obviously not the stuff of which concerts are made.'

Such vitriol for an artistic expression has always puzzled and intrigued me. At its most lyrical, jazz dance can be simply beautiful and sublime; at its most venerable, it can be frightening and complex; and at its most exciting, it can be joyous and revelatory. Why would this type of art, jazz, be so clearly misunderstood and misrepresented? The real reason is that jazz is the ultimate means of individual artistic expression with no boundaries or conformities. It cannot be contained, controlled or manipulated. Jazz is simply a creative reflection of who we are and not how we are perceived to be.

It must be remembered that jazz has always evolved through exploration, as a means of natural expression and creative output. In the first part of the twentieth century, jazz dance was not a recipient of financial support, such as sponsorship or arts' funding, and, therefore, very few theatres and dance houses looked to programme artistic jazz dance theatre. Consequently, jazz developed a populist approach more often linked to commercial enter-

BOP Company performing *Footprints in Jazz*. BAFANA SOLOMAN MATEA

tainment. This has meant that many learned critics and commentators often derided and criticized jazz as a trivial, populist form of entertainment, holding little artistic merit. Despite this, creatives have continued to create using the jazz art form as a means to share their own individual artistic expression. The fact that jazz dance has survived and thrived and continues to reinvent as a dance form is testament to its inimitable spirit.

The linage and artistic expression of jazz dance offers much to the dancer and creative practitioner. However, it is up to us as individual dancers to find a clear artistic route and creative connection to the root essence of jazz dance. In order to create and perform jazz dance at any level, we need an awareness of all the techniques and styles that are prevalent in this great art form.

Present-day jazz practitioners know that jazz dance is every bit as creative, expressive and important as contemporary and classical dance. Therefore, it is fundamental that this diverse and inspirational art form continues to be explored, expressed, understood and appreciated. More now than ever, there is a need to articulate that jazz dance is more than just a string of unrelated steps, tricks and the show of jazz hands.

This *Essential Guide to Jazz Dance* provides an overview of the history and journey of the jazz art form and brings into focus the core relationship and correlation between both the dance and the music of jazz. The book offers a comprehensive insight to the core aesthetics of the jazz vernacular, the transition and development of jazz dance, the jazz innovators and creative artists who have influenced, and continue to influence, the practice and development of jazz dance through to our present day.

Included within the pages of this book are over 200 photographs that visually support the practical value of studying jazz dance, alongside detailed resource and research material, an overview of the history of jazz music and useful practical tips and creative guides. The book is intended to support dance teachers and choreographers, dance creatives and performers, and dance enthusiasts, who find themselves interested and connected to the artistic and creative essence of jazz dance and its inherent music.

The hope is that some of the many questions from dancers, dance teachers and young jazz creatives can in some way be answered in this *Essential Guide to Jazz Dance*. In this book, by exposing and exploring the many branches and exponents of the jazz dance idiom, we hope to shine a brighter light on the jazz dance story and help to re-establish a creditable link to its incredible history, lineage and practices, so as to preserve and continue to develop this unique artistic and creative expression we call jazz dance.

CHAPTER 1

AN HISTORICAL JOURNEY

The Roots and Lineage of Jazz Dance

IN THE BEGINNING, THERE WAS A FOUR-LETTER WORD KNOWN AS 'JAZZ'

As you would expect of any great art form, the journey of jazz dance is complex, often surprising, but always inspiring and enlightening. Jazz dance did not just suddenly appear fully formed in our dance curriculums, or on the stage in musicals, theatre dance or even in pop music videos.

Understanding the history of jazz dance is vital for so many reasons. Without history (through which we acquire an understanding of technique, form and style), many dancers and practitioners have little to draw inspiration from, to inform their own development and further their practice. Historical and practical knowledge informs and connects each of us to a comprehensive understanding of the jazz dance idiom. This can only enable the dancer, teacher and choreographer a more precise understanding through which to deliver and execute the jazz dance aesthetic.

Research and knowledge through education and further professional training, is part of the package in gaining the essential skills and tools to become proficient in a chosen dance. This is no different for the jazz dancer. The more we are informed about an art form, the more we can be enlightened and inspired. As a dancer, teacher and choreographer, developing a greater appreciation and appraisal of the jazz lineage provides a superior resource from which to access and to apply one's own individual jazz dance journey.

OPPOSITE: **Melvin LeBlanc performing as 'Adam' from BOP repertoire *Daughters of Eve.*** BAFANA SOLOMAN MATEA

IN THEIR OWN WORDS...

To be proficient in any specific or chosen art form, one needs to know the history, the journey of the specific creative expression and aesthetic in question.

Dollie Henry

At its root, jazz is a celebratory art form that stems primarily from the creative aesthetics and expression of African music and dance. The transportation of African slaves via the Caribbean then on to America, introduced African musical and cultural traditions, songs and dances to the cultural and social pathways of America. Added to the melting pot was the migration of the British, Irish, Scottish and other Europeans who settled in America, bringing with them their own cultural dance traditions of clog dances, folk dances and social step dances. From different worlds and from different circumstances the African aesthetic and elements of the European aesthetic fused and amalgamated to create the only original art-form of the twentieth century. Herein lies the true source, heart and soul of this amazing art form and vernacular that we call jazz dance.

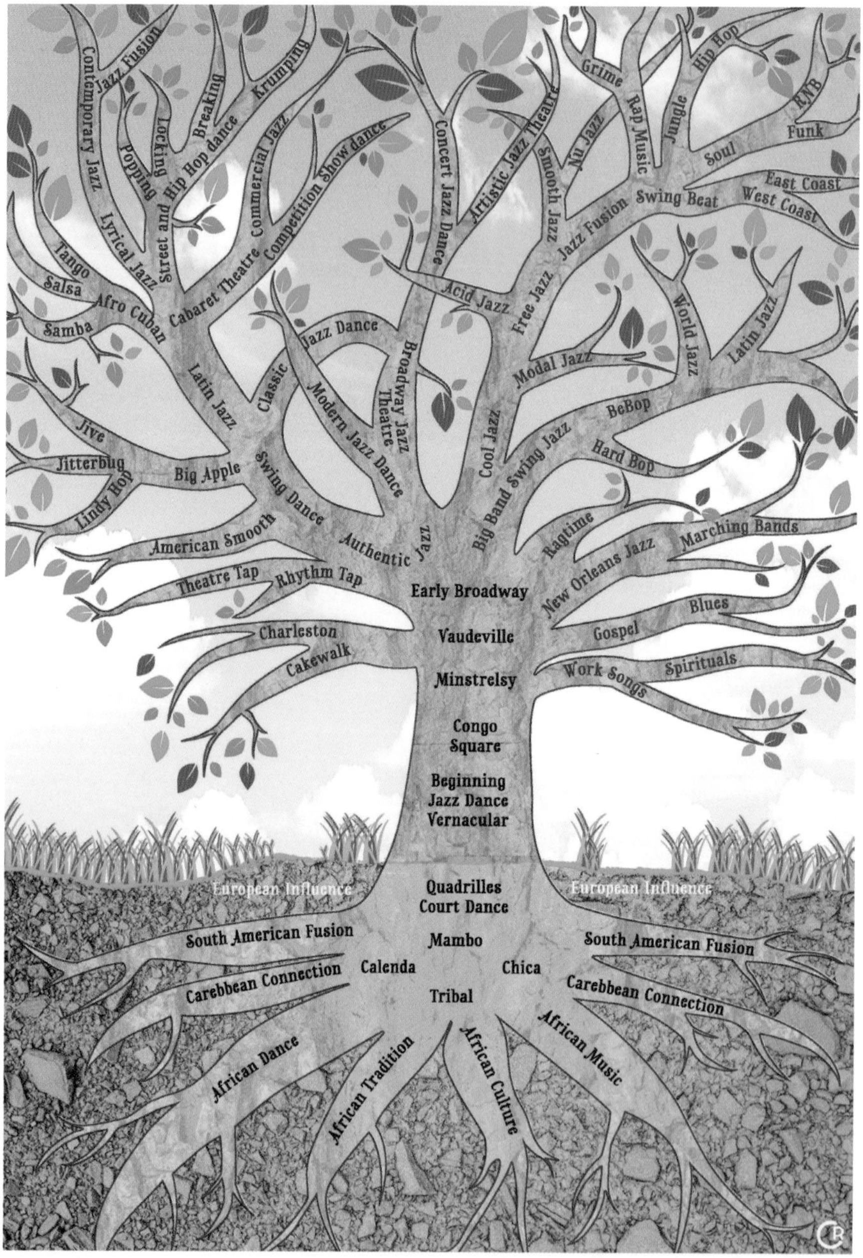

The metaphoric tree and branches of jazz. Artwork and design by Camilla Rugini.

Metaphorically, the symbol of the jazz idiom is like that of an old tree: the roots through which this incredible organic art form has been able to blossom, producing many branches that continue to reflect the diverse and creative expressions that is the jazz idiom.

The jazz tree offers a simple guideline of the growth and expansion of the jazz dance (vernacular) and the journey of its creative partner jazz music. The roots of the jazz tree run deep, the origins of the jazz idiom have germinated and transported an organic and ever-growing expression, with each branch producing a new hybrid to the lineage and practice of the jazz art form.

THE RISING ROOTS OF THE JAZZ TREE

The roots of jazz dance can be seen as amalgamation of four distinct but differing cultural and social traditions.

1. The African roots
2. The Caribbean connection
3. The South American influence
4. The European infusion

The African Root of Jazz Dance

One of the main creative foundations of jazz dance derives from African traditional and ceremonial dances. The African dance aesthetic is evident through much of early jazz dance expression and forms the foundation for the aesthetic (technical) and kinetic (physical) expression of delivery. Music is the fundamental creative seed that drives the dance and interpretation of movement. Not forgetting that the purpose behind the African tradition is a collective expression through which the dance

Mecca Vazie Andrews displaying the African dance expression. Adam Parson Commonality Dance Company, Zurich, Switzerland.

ADAM PARSON

and the music are a natural extension and creative reflection of everyday life, real life.

Throughout Africa, all tribes have their own individual dances and traditions, which are passed down to each generation. Dance and music are not separated from everyday life; they are party to all sacred and social functions, and the creative underpinning of the community.

African dance is complete in its delivery. It is performed by the community to celebrate birth, weddings, death and the marking of rites of passage. Competitive dance (challenges/battles) is also part of the structure, the re-telling of ancestral history or poetry (griots) and finding a closer connection to God (spiritual). There is a great emphasis on the collective and the community, allowing for audience and performers to participate and contribute to the whole experience (inclusive). African dance is all-inclusive and is recognized and reflected as both a sacred and secular form of cultural and creative expression.

Regina Eigbe illustrating the athleticism of a jazz jump influenced by the African dance aesthetic.

The Physical and Kinetic Characteristics

African dance cannot be viewed as one simple form of dance expression. There are many differences between the tribal groups and regional dances of Africa, which dictate the dances' physical aesthetic and delivery.

Each region of African dance has a specific emphasis on the physical expression and movement. For example, in Ghana, the upper body is a predominant feature within the physical movement. In regions such as Nigeria, the emphasis is accentuated through hips and pelvis. The African tribe of the Maasai are known for their athletic legs, jumps and elevation, and then there is the intricate footwork and hand clapping that is akin to the Akan traditions of Ghana.

African dance has three distinct attributes:

1. **Polyrhythmics** – the connectivity between the physical expression and interpretation of dance movement to the intricate, crossed rhythms and accents within the music.
2. **Polycentrism** – denotes the dexterity to subdivide the body movements, using differing parts of the body at the same time. This quality is aligned to the differing layers and sounds in the music and musical instrumentation.
3. **Improvisation** – the immediate expression of dance and movement without preparation, creating a spontaneous physical and emotional connection and individual creative expression to the music.

These are recognizable attributes in the physical expression of African dance. However, it is through the relationship to the music that the dance takes on another direction of energy, communication and connectivity. The core essence of African creative culture and tradition is through dance and music, which are innately and instinctively connected and part of everyday life.

Students learning African dance movement.

African dance is very versatile in conception and execution. There are no restrictions to the body and physical movement; therefore, African dance can be presented and performed in varying ways: from slow and controlled in movement (lyrical), to the most spontaneous and dynamic of movement, evolving through intuitive performance (improvisation). The dance can also be performed to show power and strength (warrior/tribal dances), to offering a peaceful transition in death and honouring the Gods (ceremonial and ring dances). This is bound together through acknowledging cultural traditions that strengthens the bond within the community (storytelling/singing/call and response).

The Caribbean Connection

The Caribbean geographically is a group of islands in the Caribbean Sea that spans over the south-east of the Gulf of Mexico, east of Central America and north of South America. It includes the islands of Cuba, Hispaniola, Haiti, Jamaica, Grenada, Carriacou Dominican Republic, Trinidad and Tobago and many others.

Caribbean dance evolved from complex influences, due to European colonization of the islands by the British, French, Spanish, Portuguese and Dutch. It followed that the indigenous folk dances would certainly be influenced by European dance styles and music. The Africans, brought to work on the plantations, continued to hold on to their creative customs and drumming traditions, but also adopted the dances of the indigenous population on the Islands. The indigenous people of some of the Islands, called Arawaks or the Taino people, originated from mainland South America, but found homelands on the islands of the Caribbean. The traditional dances that are still observed on the islands include the kumina and tambu from Jamaica, the bele from Martinique and, from Haiti, the voodoo dances.

Calinda, dance of the Negróes in America. Artist François Aimé Louis Dumoulin.

Through the dances and music of the Caribbean, the direct lineage to the traditions and connections of African dance and music continued to live. Plantation dances, such as the bamboula, juba, voodoo, calinda and the chica, were slave dances performed on the plantations by both men and women.

European dances taken to the Islands include the quadrilles, square dances, cotillions, alongside the more courtly or classical dances of the time, such as the gavotte, minuet and sarabande. The Caribbean islands that danced the quadrille continued to evidence the traditional dances and customs directly linked to Africa, by developing their own characteristic adaptations. The structure gave rise to many versions of the Caribbean quadrille.

The South American Influence

It is sometimes forgotten that African slaves were transported to both North and South America. It was the Portuguese who began the forced movement of African slaves to Brazil and other parts of South America throughout the sixteenth century. The African traditions and cultural expressions, musical rhythms and physical aesthetics resonate throughout Latin American dance forms. The dances recognizable from this region of the world include the rumba, a style of dance that originates from the musical pulse of the African drum. It is a fast-moving, hip-swinging and competitive dance, always accompanied by fast-paced drum music, alongside more traditional Latin instruments, such as maracas, the clave and shakers. Over time this evolved into the chica dance. The chica dance has a direct lineage to the Africa tribal dances of the Congo. It was a dance performed for processions (marching) and religious ceremonies. A descendent of the chica dance is the dance of the fandango. The mamba (also called 'mambo' meaning 'conversation with the gods') originated in Cuba from the Haitians of African descendants. The mamba is a spiritual and religious dance and music ceremony and tradition that evokes the spirit 'voodoo' of the high priestess mamba.

It is important to recognize that much of African dance had a specific meaning. Consequently, the power of this type of dance enabled the survival of the African and Caribbean traditions, both in dance

Marie Antoinette by creator Johann Georg Weigert. PUBLIC DOMAIN: WIKIMEDIA COMMONS

BELOW: ***A Gypsy Dance in the Gardens of the Alcázar* 1851. Artist Alfred Dehodencq. This is a faithful photographic reproduction of a two-dimensional public domain of art (PD-Art 1923).**

and music. This can be clearly recognized today in most Afro-Latin dance styles, including the samba, merengue and calypso. The social dance element continues to keep the Latin connection very much part of the jazz journey, both for the non-professional and professional dancer.

The European Infusion

European dance is traditionally viewed as a secular and status art form. The development and practice of the dances descend from two distinctive styles of dance and expression: court/classical dances (upper class) and folk dances (lower class).

Classical dance (ballet) first appeared in the Italian courts of the sixteenth century and then became popular in France during the reign of Louis XIV. Much of the dance technique formed in the seventeenth century set in place the origins of classical dance. Among the formal courtly dances from Baroque and Renaissance dance of the seventeenth century were the minuet, gavotte, waltz, quadrille or contredanse and cotillion.

Folk dances of European descent that originate from the indigenous people are recognized as informal dances, such as the clog dances, Irish jig, morris dance, pole dancing, Scottish lilts, polka, gypsy and flamenco dance. These dances were often perceived as non-technical dances of the working-class community.

An interesting observation is that the European court dances presented a visual non-transferable expression, whilst folk dance presented a physical and creative expression of the community – no different in purpose to that of the traditional African dances.

In conclusion, the roots of jazz dance can easily be identified by the three-dance expression: African dance, South American dance and European dance. Each offers something unique, yet wholly individual, to the jazz dance story. It is from this unique social interaction and cross-fertilization that the jazz vernacular has been afforded a foundation from which to grow, over time developing into one of the most popular and influential dance forms of the past two hundred plus years.

CONGO SQUARE – THE BIRTHPLACE OF THE JAZZ VERNACULAR

From the late eighteenth century, southern America was a melting pot of different world cultures, from Africa, the Caribbean, South America and Europe. In particular, Congo Square in New Orleans was to become a pivotal location for the development of

BOP residency participants in the creative process working through connection and energy between each other.

African musical instruments.

the early jazz vernacular. Every Sunday at Congo Square the enslaved Africans would be given free time to come together as a people, to share and express their customs and traditions through music, song and dance. At these Congo Square gatherings, music of African rhythms, syncopation and accented beats (polyrhythms) provided an accompaniment to the traditional African spiritual and ceremonial dances and songs. Instruments in use at that time would have consisted of African drums and banjos, alongside hand and body clapping (patting juba) and vocals. This immediate creative expression through the connection between the dancer and musician became the underlying principle of the jazz idiom, namely improvisation. This exchange of ideas provided an organic creative interaction between the dancers and musicians and offered a form of entertainment to the gathered crowds.

The drive of the rhythms created by the African musicians was fundamental to the movement and shaping of the dance. The rhythms of African music established the natural swing beat recognized by the 2/4 timing, different to the more usual 3/4 time-signature of European classical music. This difference in time-signatures is an important aspect in defining the rhythmic pulse, timing and physical expression of jazz dance, which are part and parcel of African music and dance traditions.

The early development of the jazz vernacular was influenced by dance steps and movements that can be recognized from the traditional African-American dance vocabulary and accompanying music. Unfortunately, many of the specific African dance steps have been lost over time and are certainly not evident in much of modern-day jazz dance.

However, some have survived and, although the original meaning and techniques may have been lost, they are still an important part of the jazz dance legacy. Many of the original dance steps and styles have not survived the journey, but some of the more authentic steps and movements have evolved, allowing other derivative jazz dance styles to develop, these include:

- The ring shout
- Patting juba
- Cakewalk
- Charleston
- Hooffin'
- Tap dance
- The shuffle
- Turkey trot
- Buzzard lope
- Truckin'

In parallel with the African dance aesthetic were the European dance influences. Throughout the eighteenth and nineteenth centuries, millions of European migrants emigrated to America bringing with them their own dances, music and cultural nuances. Many of these dances represented not only the social status, but also the cultural identity of each country or region; for example, the waltz and minuet (court dances) and the clog dances of the north of England and the Scottish reel from the Highlands (folk dances).

European dances included:

- The Irish jig
- The Scottish lilt
- The Lancashire clog dance
- The hornpipe
- Gypsy dances
- Square dances
- Minuet
- Waltz

The dances and music of African traditions, infused with the European traditions, were to emancipate a unique style of dance and music. Fundamentally, it is from these early encounters between displaced

Late nineteenth-century artist's conception of African dances several generations earlier. Engraving by E. W. Kemble, to illustrate article 'The Dance in Place Congo, New Orleans' by George Washington Cable, published in *Century Magazine*, February 1886.

cultures and traditions that the beginnings of a new art form of jazz dance was to be shaped and developed.

IN THEIR OWN WORDS...

In *The Story of American Vernacular Dance*, by Marshall and Jean Stearns, they describe the new dance founded in New Orleans as a vernacular or homegrown dance – the beginnings of jazz.

MOVING THROUGH THE MINSTRELSY ERA

This new American dance vernacular (jazz) was to rise to prominence through the minstrelsy era.

The concept of minstrel shows emerged from the pre-industrial European traditions of courtly dress, facial masking and festivals, and was created, initially, as a form of community and social entertainment. In America during the 1800s, the popularity of this form of entertainment developed widespread appeal. Minstrelsy was a form of entertainment initially devised for travelling tent and gillie shows that toured from town to town – review shows that provided social commentary and entertainment to the mass public. The show format was further formalized, transforming the concept into the most popular form of public entertainment in America.

The creative architecture of the minstrel style and movement was heavily influenced by black creative and cultural expression. As a direct consequence of this popularity, and the undeniable flair of African-American dance and music, white promotors and performers saw an opportunity to commercially exploit a new style of minstrelsy entertainment. This resulted in the beginnings of the blackface minstrel show.

One of the first documented professional blackface minstrels was the dancer John Durang (1768–1822). He was said to have made famous the use of the hornpipe within his dance and, in 1789, he appeared as a blackface performer, helping to popularize blackface minstrelsy. Another name that is well recorded in the jazz history books, and recognized for accelerating blackface minstrelsy, was a white New Yorker and comedian called Thomas Dartmouth aka Daddy Rice. Daddy Rice created a blackface character, taking his inspiration from African expression and aesthetic. Dartmouth created a song and dance parody called Jump Jim Crow. Daddy Rice and his performance of Jump Jim Crow, both as a song and as a dance act, became

Cover to early edition of *Jump Jim Crow* sheet music. Thomas D. Rice is pictured in his blackface role performing at the Bowery Theatre (also known as the American Theatre) at the time. This image was highly influential on later Jim Crow and minstrelsy images. 1 January 1832.

a huge success and as a performer he went on to gain further infamy performing throughout America. Dartmouth also gained recognition and further prominence performing in London and Dublin in the late 1800s.

Blackface minstrelsy continued unabated, with white performers blackening their faces (with burnt cork), imitating and adopting the musical flair, mannerisms and dance movements, by way of caricature and parody, of the African-American slaves.

This was the reality of the times in America and it is important to acknowledge and place the facts in context. It is, therefore, not surprising that one of the consequences of the historical and political circumstances of America during the rise of the minstrelsy tradition, is that much of the history of the black originators of the jazz vernacular are lost

Al G. Field Minstrels poster print, *c.* 1910 by Otis Lithograph Co Image.

in time or simply do not exist as part of early jazz dance history.

Today we may view the early minstrelsy era with a heavy heart, as clearly this type of entertainment was heavily based on racial stereotypes and racist sentiment. However repugnant this may feel, it is clear that the music, dance, creative flair and ingenuity of the black creative expression, greatly influenced the minstrelsy era and the original foundations of the jazz dance aesthetic.

Although it might seem that the concept of minstrelsy was generally only performed by white entertainers mocking and adopting black expression, this was far from the truth. As early as the 1850s, the performance landscape saw the rise in popularity of black minstrel troupes.

In much the same way that white performers mocked the black slave, the black performers created a style of dance to mock the white elite. This was characterized by assimilating the highbrow persona and posture of their white counterparts, combined with the intricate footwork and physicality of African dance and rhythmic musical timing. This parody of performance was to become a very popular and sought-after form of black minstrel entertainment. One of the early dances that originated from this imitation exchange was the cakewalk.

As the minstrelsy concept grew, and the shows became larger and grander, female performers were introduced and later became featured as dancers and singers. Blues and spiritual singers Bessie Smith and Ma Rainey began their performing careers as performers in the minstrel shows. By the start of the twentieth century, the bigger minstrel companies would employ both white and black performers. This resulted in a more acceptable platform for white audiences to view the talent and performances of black performers.

England was also privy to the minstrelsy popularity of America. Famous black minstrels who found notoriety as performers in Britain included The Bohee Brothers, Billy Kersands and Master Juba, alongside Bert Williams and George Walker. Williams was a significant performer in the advancement of African-American musical and pantomime theatre. Following on from minstrelsy, he became one of vaudeville's top artists, with his solo performances and also as part of the double-act 'Williams and Walker'.

Williams and Walker developed into important creative performing artists. It was through their unique approach to theatre, along with their skills in performing, comedy, singing and dancing, that they went on to write and star in their own off-Broadway shows. Part of their act was to introduce the authentic jazz dance of the cakewalk into mainstream theatre entertainment. Williams was to become the first black entertainer to take a lead role on the Broadway stage and he also performed with the renowned Ziegfeld Follies.

As white minstrel shows grew in scale, black minstrel shows began to grow too, adding other traditional elements, such as spirituals and religious songs to their performances and acts. This creative expression resonated more directly with their own black audiences and, at the same time, informed and drew in white audiences.

Part of the success of minstrelsy was due to effective business management evident through lucrative touring circuits that were set up under the Theatre Owners Booking Association aka TOBA and also The Chitlin Circuit. This assisted the rise in popularity of both white and black minstrelsy, taking it from the southern states to the northern states of America.

In many ways, minstrelsy is a double-edged concept of entertainment. On the one hand, it brought the black expression of dance and music to a wider and more diverse national demographic. However, on the other hand, it was the beginning of mass appropriation of black populist creative art and a delineation that still resonates within the commercial aspects of populist entertainment of today.

THE RISE OF VAUDEVILLE

The vaudeville era came straight off the back of minstrelsy. In the latter part of the nineteenth century, and into the twentieth century, the sway

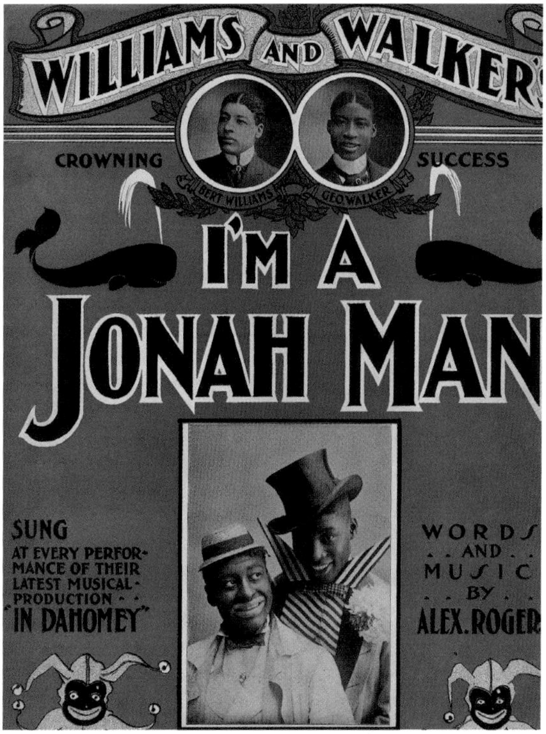

'I'm a Jonah Man' from the musical *In Dahomey*, 1903 sheet music cover. Bert Williams and George Walker, vaudeville stars 'Williams and Walker', shown on cover in both formal portraits and in stage costumes with blackface.

of minstrelsy was diminishing. Vaudeville was to become the new platform for performers and creators, and a greater variety of popular entertainment.

The format of vaudeville was designed to showcase a series of differing acts grouped together to create a full variety show. The shows would present and combine acts that included musicians, vocalists and dance acts, alongside comedians, magicians, impersonators, acrobats and circus acts. Vaudeville offered a major source of entertainment that brought the jazz expression and the early stages of theatre entertainment to the masses. Most large towns in the USA sited vaudeville houses and the touring circuits grew ever popular, allowing many more acts to perform throughout the country. The fascination of vaudeville as a form of entertainment was that it was able to cross all generations and offered an inclusive appeal to audiences, bringing all ethnicities together on stage and in the audience.

Vaudeville became the starting place for the careers of many artists, who rose to fame and attained international star status in their various forms as actors, singers, dancers, radio artists and film stars. Iconic names such as Al Jolson, James Cagney, Charlie Chaplin, Fred Astaire and his sister Adele, Josephine Baker, Bill BoJangles, the Nicholas Brothers, Pearl Bailey, Ma Rainey and Sammy Davis Jr, all found their way into entertainment through vaudeville.

The vaudeville era did not last beyond the American Depression. By mid-1930s radio and film were to become the new forms of social entertainment and with that, jazz expression and vernacular was to reform and take new directions of development.

EARLY AUTHENTIC JAZZ DANCE STYLES

In the early 1900s, jazz vernacular and form were finding a niche as an accepted form of social and cultural expression. Many of the authentic steps and styles, recognized as social dances, are part of the jazz dance lineage today. Even if diluted, certain steps and styles and formations can be traced back to some of the original jazz dance forms. For example:

- Cakewalk
- Tap dance
- Charleston
- Black bottom
- The big apple

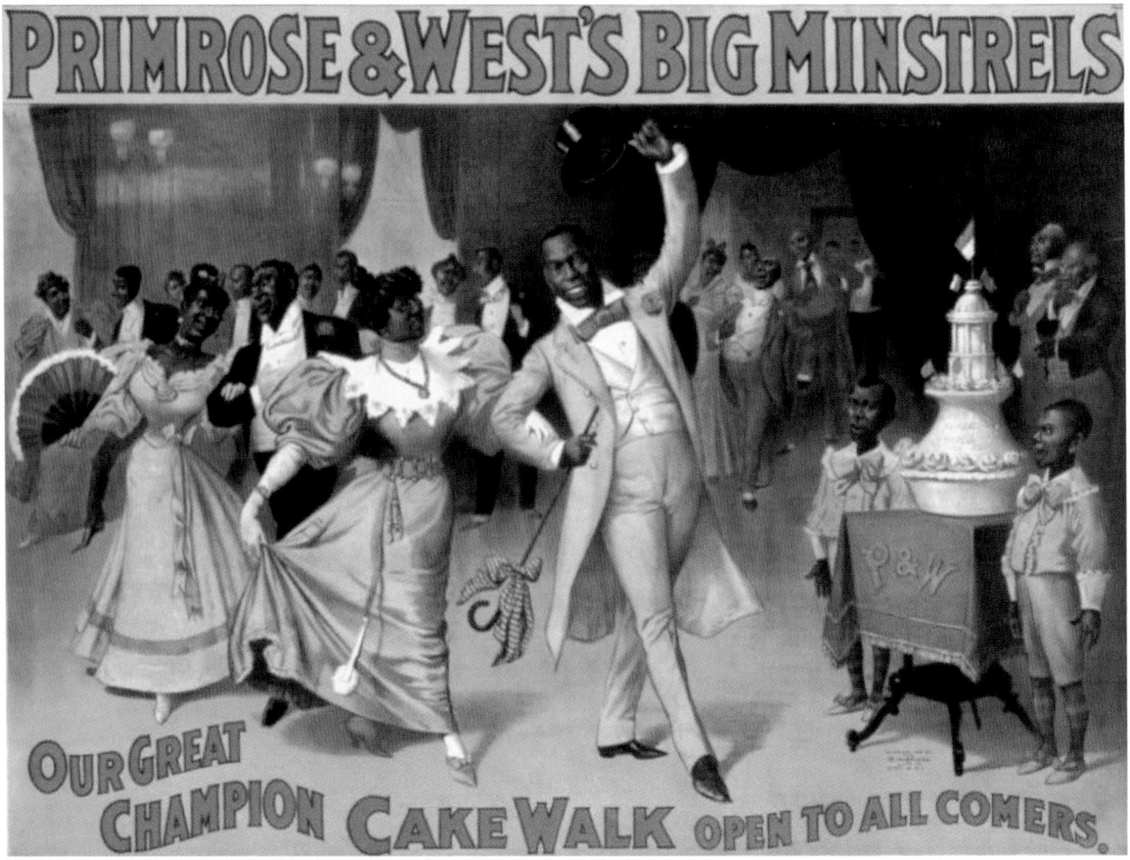

'Primrose and West's Big Minstrels. Our great champion cake walk, open to all comers. 1896'. Strobridge Lithographing Co., Cincinnati and New York.

- Swing dance
- Lindy-hop dance
- Foxtrot

The Cakewalk

The cakewalk was originally viewed and performed as early as 1850, as a competitive plantation dance. The cakewalk displays a style of movement that is energetic and fast-paced. It was originally known as the chalk line walk on the Southern plantations and later became widely known as the cakewalk.

In essence, the cakewalk was an exaggerated parody, created by the slaves to imitate the upper-class mannerisms of their white plantation-owners and their formal social dances. The main figures of movement and steps derived from European dances, such as the minuet. The upper part of the body was positioned more upright and formal in stature and deportment. The bottom half of the body, in contrast, was much more physical with high leg kicks, walking (high-stepping) and parading to the 2/4 time musical signature that accompanied the dance. To this was added improvisation by the dancer, showing an individual flair of physicality and dance prowess.

In has been documented that as Sunday entertainment, plantation-owners would present special competitions to show who had the best slave cake-walker. As a prize, a cake was given to the best individual dancer or dancing couple. The cakewalk, as a dance, blossomed way beyond the plantation confines in popularity and, as a consequence, became a prominent dance in style and content. The dance was introduced into the minstrel shows and, by the late 1890s, the cakewalk became an extremely popular dance style.

The Charleston

The Charleston as a dance style is still very recognizable in jazz dance vocabulary. As a new dance, the Charleston was seen as early as 1903 and is a fusion of both African and European dance styles. The Charleston is a feisty, high-octane dance, generally performed to the music of ragtime in 4/4 time and has been referred to as the improvisor's dance. Physically, the lower half of the body (the feet) moves to the specific musical beats with flick kicks and turns, and the upper part of the body is left free to use hand gestures and more accentuated arm movements. The Charleston is a dance that can be performed as a solo, in couples partnering or as a group.

The Charleston dance also had a pivotal mark on the fashion of the day, by introducing the flapper dress. The style and design became a fashion statement and a form of outward expression for women. Competition platforms allowed for the dance to further develop as its popularity grew. Eventually, the Charleston found its way into revue shows at the famous Cotton Club. In these types of shows, dance was always accompanied by the music of jazz. The Charleston even made its way onto the Broadway stage and found prominence in the all-black musical called *Runnin' Wild* (1923). This production was to feature a song also entitled *The Charleston*. The

Josephine Baker dancing the Charleston at Folies-Bergère, Paris Review Show, La Folie du Jour Dance 1926. Image by Walery French 1863–1935.

Charleston managed to cross both the musical and dance worlds and continued to play a big part in the jazz dance journey.

The Big Apple

It is suggested that the big apple originates from the religious dance performed by African Americans on plantations in South Carolina called the ring shout. The dance itself was named after the juke joint called Big Apple, which is where the dance was first performed. The dance is based on the figure and form of the African ring shout, which is performed as a group in the formation of a circle.

The big apple is based on the call and response, the genetic DNA of African dance tradition. The dance has a caller who 'calls out' to the next dancer or couple who will enter the centre of the group circle and perform an improvised dance response. After the Charleston, the big apple was to become the next jazz dance trend and a social dance that both the black and white youth dancers would develop into the dance mainstream.

The Lindy-Hop

The style of lindy-hop is one of the most recognized jazz dance styles with the technique still practised and performed in its original form today. The lindy-hop came out of the dance scene in Harlem. The dance itself is a hybrid of the Charleston and big apple, which were created on the dance floor at venues such as the Savoy Ballroom.

The lindy-hop is sometimes called the jitterbug and is the original form of swing dance that evolved in the 1920s. The dance style was adaptable and developed to interpret and reflect the music as it changed from what was known as hot jazz of the late 1920s to the big swing bands of the 1930s. As is the jazz way, it was the dancers and performers who continued to develop the lindy-hop dance style, always making sure that the dance had a close creative relationship with the music.

As the lindy-hop developed through its initial fusion with the syncopated moves of the Charleston, other specific dance steps were added. These included the Susie Q, trukkin' and swing o' alongside, the partnering content of the break away and the athleticism of flash aerial lifts. Maintaining its link to the big apple, the lindy-hop also used the formation of a circle, known as the jam circle. The circle formation allowed the performers to take the centre spot to show their particular individual improvisational flair or partnering skills.

One of the difficulties when studying the history and legacy of jazz dance, is that not much recorded media was either produced or survived. The style and techniques of this great art form were, throughout its first 100 years, passed down from performer to performer. The early twentieth century changed all that as recorded media slowly developed. Obviously, in jazz music we have the early New Orleans recordings of the 1920s to anchor the history. In jazz dance it was not until film production became more popular that early jazz dance forms and styles began to be documented. It is, therefore, not surprising that the names we often remember as pioneers of jazz dance are often those that can reference documentary evidence. One such individual was Shorty George.

The Pioneers of the Lindy-Hop

The first pioneer and most popular lindy-hop dancer of the time was 'Shorty George' Snowden (4 July 1904–May 1982). Shorty George was an acclaimed dancer at the Savoy Ballroom where he performed from its opening in 1927. At only five feet tall, Snowden crafted his act around his height as a featuring asset for his dance and style. He worked in partnership with the dancer Big Bea (she was much taller than him). Through entering dance competitions and developing their double act, they inspired a new form of partner dance. Shorty George went on to set up the first professional lindy-hop troupe called 'The Shorty Snowden Dancers' and bring fame to his signature step called the 'Shorty George', which continues to be a signature step of lindy-hop today.

Another name who brought authentic jazz dance to a new level of recognition was dancer and choreographer Frankie Manning (1914–99). From the mid-1930s, swing dancer Frankie Manning became a leading dancer at Harlem's Savoy Ballroom. After

Shorty George, he went on to revolutionize the dance of the lindy-hop with his innovative choreography and his highly coordinated, syncronized ensemble lindy routines. As a featured dancer and main choreographer for the renowned dance group the Whitey's Lindy Hoppers, Manning and his group went on to perform in numerous Hollywood films; one that sticks out as a favourite is *Hellzapoppin'*. As a group, they became well established and found success performing on stages worldwide. Frankie Manning was a dance innovator of his time and introduced dance steps that allowed the movement

Lindy-hop performers and swing dance creatives Jreena Green and Shango (UK). ANNALISA BANELLO

of dance to interpret the swing music of jazz bands of the era. The dance group worked closely with jazz composers and bandleaders such as Duke Ellington, Cab Calloway to Count Basie and supported jazz singers Ethel Waters and Ella Fitzgerald.

Manning was able to bring together all the social dance moves and techniques from the past and fuse them with his own unique style of the lindy-hop. He created with his dancers a new and dynamic style of jazz dance that required a superior technique, physical dexterity and flair from the performers.

Frankie Manning and his legacy, as one of the innovators of lindy-hop and swing dance, lives on today through the many lindy-hop dancers and swing dance groups still practising and performing the form worldwide. From the clubs to the Savoy Ballroom and through the decades, the lindy-hop has survived and is the hybrid of all the early social dances that led to the next evolution of jazz dance and the forerunner for the swing dance era.

Swing Dance

The swing in jazz dance is still with us today. Swing from a historic view point is often represented as a style of jazz music from which the dance evolved. Swing refers to the musical beat and rhythm derived from African music traditions. Interestingly, swing is also often talked about in music circles as that indefinable quality of jazz timing that signals a great performer. As the jazz music pioneer, Duke Ellington, wrote, 'It don't mean a thing if it ain't got that swing'.

Swing dance is a fusion and extension of the dances lindy-hop, big apple and Charleston. Its relationship with the jazz music of the day, swing music, was paramount, as the dance was a reflection of the timings and rhythms of swing jazz.

During the 1930s to the late 1940s, the rise and popularity of swing big bands allowed swing dance to become the new social dance that was adopted by all racial and cultural communities. From the West Coast to the East Coast of America, the dance reflected the differing dance styles that were adapted; where performers displayed dance that was a representation of the region. For example, in the West Coast, they used the dance and footwork taken from the Charleston, fox trot and jig trot, whilst on the East Coast and in the Southern regions of America, they created their own style of the swing dance that used the older two-step based dance form.

Just like the previous social dances, the partnering aspect is a prominent feature of swing dance. Swing dance was to influence other jazz dance styles such the jive. The popularity of swing dance was also adopted into the dance scene in Europe, becoming a dance craze and social gathering that continues today, with many professional and amateur swing dancers and swing dance events.

As jazz dance grew out of a social environment, dance competitions provided important social events that had considerable influence and development on many aspects of the jazz dance aesthetic. These competitions fostered highly creative performers through which many of the more innovative dance movements originated and developed. These moves and tricks would eventually find their way into the commercial dance arena, slowly being absorbed into much of the popular dance entertainment of the day.

It is evident that jazz dance peaked in popularity during the swing era. The jazz music of swing and the jazz dance of swing complemented each other perfectly, both driving the other through a journey of creative and artistic development. As the swing era drew to a close and jazz music moved on to more complicated forms of expression through bebop, the symbiotic relationship between jazz music and jazz dance was broken. This is not to say that jazz music no longer had an influence over the development of jazz dance. It simply meant that jazz dancers and creatives had to seek out new forms of jazz music that had a greater connection with dance movement and choreography.

The authentic jazz dance styles of the lindy-hop, Charleston and swing dance, and their innovative and cultural origins, have stood the test of time and are still very much a part of, and still influence, the expression and aesthetic of jazz dance.

Lindy-hop and swing performers Jreena Green and Shango (UK). ANNALISA BANELLO

CHAPTER 2

TAP DANCE

First Cousin of the Jazz Vernacular

THE TALKING FEET OF TAP

Tap dance is an essential root of the jazz dance tree and its significance cannot be under-estimated. Fundamentally, tap dance is a unique expression of rhythmic musical interpretation and, in essence, is a form of communication and conversation between the dancer and the music or 'call and response'.

The feet are the primary source of executing the syncopated and rhythmic creative transference between the dancer and the music. Tap draws from its lineage a fusion and combination of West African tribal steps and movements, derived from the dances of the juba and ring shout, performed with percussion instruments.

In parallel, European social and folk dances, such as the Irish jig, Scottish lilt and Lancashire clog dances, alongside the influences of Spanish gypsy dances, have all had a part to play in the story of tap dance.

In its infancy tap dance developed wholly from its innate relationship to the music through improvised delivery and can be identified as the earliest form of authentic jazz dance. Tap dance rose from the slave plantations and street corners, on to the platforms of minstrelsy and vaudeville, and into Broadway musicals and films. Tap dance is the first recognizable dance form (vernacular) in the jazz journey.

One of the original tap dance pioneers was black performer William Henry Lane, also known as Master

OPPOSITE: **Aleksandr Ostanin, rhythmic tap choreographer and performer (Ukraine).**
YURIY BOCHKAREV

Lancashire clog shoes.

Juba, who produced an early tap dance style that combined the aesthetic of the African juba dance and the European Irish jig. The dance juba (djouba or gioube) is a style of dance noted as extremely dynamic with emphasis of rhythms placed through feet (stomping), hand-clapping and body patting, using the body as a drum.

As early as the mid-1800s, Master Juba was recognized as one of the main catalysts for tap dance and a star attraction in minstrel shows. Lane is a key player in revealing tap dance as a primary expression of the jazz vernacular. He founded his career in the clubs and music halls of Manhattan, New York. During his lifetime, Master Juba became an international sensation, noted for performing many times in London with Pell's Ethiopian Serenaders, which included appearances at the then famous Vauxhall Gardens, London.

William Henry Lane, aka 'Master Juba' from *The Illustrated London News*, 5 August 1848. Scanned copy from *Dan Emmett and the Rise of Early Negro Minstrelsy* by Hans Nathan.

IN THEIR OWN WORDS...

Authenticity is the most important thing. You have to know where it all comes from, study who pioneered it.

Savion Glover

DEFINING THE BEATS OF THE TAP VERNACULAR

As is the seed of jazz dance, it is through the relationship between the music and the dance that is key to the delivery of tap dance vocabulary, styles and dance expressions.

There are two distinct styles of tap dance that can be identified:

- **Rhythm tap** (authentic jazz dance/rhythm tap) – the focus is on the connection and improvisation to jazz music. The dancer looks to develop tap vocabulary through interpreting and responding to jazz music, created through improvisation and originality of the performers.
- **Theatre tap** (musical theatre/show dance) – the focus is on set choreography that requires little improvisation from the dancer(s). The content and style of tap dance will generally be dictated by a specific storyline, characterization and set dance pieces, aligned to musical theatre and show dances.

IN THEIR OWN WORDS...

Your background has a lot to do with your approach to movement.

Cholly Atkins

Gumboot dance performed by mine workers in South Africa.

Rhythm Tap

Rhythm tap developed mainly through black performers. These African-American tap pioneers had a far-reaching impact on the development of both rhythmic and theatre tap, but more often than not were under-represented both in film and on Broadway. However, their magnitude and contribution to the tap dance story cannot be under-estimated.

The masters tappers or, as they were affectionately known, hoofers, were the authentic innovators of rhythm tap. The names that stand out in history include Sandman Sims, Maceo Anderson, Cholly Atkins, Honi Coles, Bill Bailey, James 'Buster' Brown, Jimmy Slyde and Sammy Davis Jr. Each has brought an individuality, immense personality and unique style of showmanship to the tap and jazz dance vernacular.

The term 'hoofer' derived from the name of a New York club establishment located in Harlem called the Hoofers Club. The gatherings allowed for much more than the creation of new tap vocabulary and exchanges of ideas. The hoofers kept alive the art of improvisation, the intuitive thread found in jazz dance and the spark from which rhythm tap and jazz dance is initially discovered.

Theatre Tap

Theatre tap developed throughout the vaudeville era and went on to find greater success in films and on Broadway. Within the confines of musical theatre, tap dance is often structured and choreographed to an inch of its life, with emphasis on executing dance movements that features set and concept-driven ensemble show tap dance and production numbers.

Broadway theatre shows of the 1930s created by Busby Berkeley and the theatrical revue shows of Florenz Ziegfeld made popular the tap chorus line with spectacular grand-scale musical dance productions that provided the glitz and glamour of theatre entertainment. Ziegfeld was to become one of the leading theatrical producers of his day and created a platform for many dancers and performers that came through vaudeville, catapulting the names of artists such as Josephine Baker, Bert Williams and Fanny Brice into the spotlight.

It is through the popularity of Hollywood film musicals that many more dancers and performers ascended to greater stardom. Fred Astaire, Ginger Rogers and Eleanor Powell, Ann Miller, Danny Kaye, Donald O'Connor, Gene Kelly and child star Shirley Temple, are just some of the more familiar names known for establishing their own particular style and impression of tap dance.

No one tap dancer is the same – each brings an individuality and style that is unique. Fred Astaire, known for his classic, refined air of elegance, was influenced by ballroom and classical dance, while Donald O'Connor provided an energetic, sporty, grounded style to his dance choreography and performance style. Both drew from the influences of African-American jazz expression and yet were completely different in their presentation and expression of tap dance.

IN THEIR OWN WORDS...

I'm basically a hoofer, a tap dancer. I was always very good from the waist down, moving with the feet.... I became what's known as a total dancer, using the entire body in order to express what you want to express in tap dancing and line.

Donald O'Connor

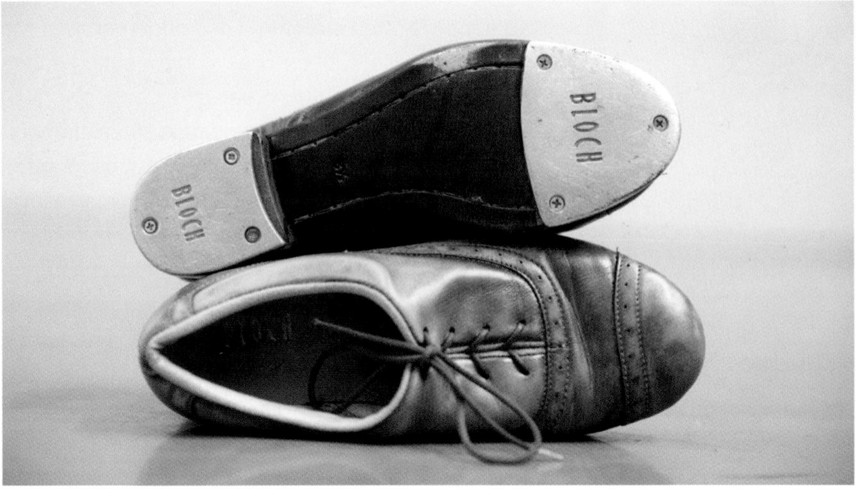

A pair of red, lived-in tap shoes.
BAFANA SOLOMAN MATEA

TAP DANCE INNOVATORS AND PIONEERS

Innovators of the tap vernacular gained further recognition and prominence in vaudeville, which opened opportunities for many speciality song and dance acts. One double-act to make a significant impact on tap dance was the song and dance duo Buck and Bubbles, real names Ford Lee Washington (Buck) and John Washington Sublett (Bubbles).

Bubbles established a unique jazz style and aesthetic for rhythmic tap dance. He was known for a style that was fast and eclectic, and noted for using offbeat and accenting tap rhythms and syncopation. Buck and Bubbles' popularity marked them as the first black musical act to perform at Radio City Music Hall and they were instrumental in opening the doors for other black artists to perform in mainstream theatres across America.

Buck and Bubbles understood the importance of staged performances and placed much emphasis on the visual aspect of their work. They presented their act wearing tuxedos and top hats, giving rise to the term 'class act'. This formal wear was worn in theatre musicals from early vaudeville to Broadway productions of Ziegfeld or Busby Berkeley, right through to our present day Broadway/West End musicals such as *42nd Street* and *Top Hat.* Fundamentally, it is a reference to the early black jazz dances, such as the cakewalk, where the performers often dressed up in their finery to present an image for their plantation owners and white audiences.

Bill 'Bojangles' Robinson (1878–1949)

The highly influential and innovative performer Bill 'Bojangles' Robinson is one of the early tap artists to be acknowledged in name as a tap dance innovator.

Bojangles was a world-class tap dancer in both buck and wing and Irish step dancing. His style of tap dance was key to his specific tap sound. His tap style was placed on his toes rather than flat-footed and heavy, suggesting a gentle and light-weighted effect to his particular dance style and tap sound. He made his name on the vaudeville circuit. His act and style brought him to the attention of producers, eventually leading to specialist feature roles in Hollywood films and musicals during the 1940s and 1950s.

IN THEIR OWN WORDS...

What success I achieved in the theater is due to the fact that I have always worked just as hard when there were ten people in the house as when there were thousands. Just as hard in Springfield, Illinois as on Broadway.

Bill (Bojangles) Robinson

Image of Bill Bojangles Robinson. Publicity photo by James Kriegsmann, New York, 23 March 1942.

The stair dance became his insignia show piece, both in live stage performances and highlighted within the films he appeared in. One of his most memorable performances is his duet with young song and dance child star Shirley Temple in the film *Little Colonel.*

The Nicholas Brothers (Fayard 1914–2006 and Harold 1921–2000)

Without doubt, the Nicholas Brothers, Fayard and Harold, together brought a truly unique and fearless energy to tap dance, topped off with an acrobatic flair and physical agility. The Nicholas Brothers created a style and technique of tap dance known as flash tap. The innovative style flash tap incorporated acrobatic dance tricks, leaps and jumps into the dance sequences to uplift and exhilarate their performance for their audiences. More importantly, flash tap as a technique was to set a new trend.

The Nicholas Brothers are without doubt one of the most recognized and influential African-American tap dance acts in jazz dance history. The Nicholas Brothers' style of tap dance and showmanship has inspired whole generations of tap dancers, although it is often said that the Nicholas Brothers' unique style has never been replicated to their level of ingenuity, technique, skill and execution. Fortunately, there are videos, documentaries and films that are available to view their spectacular performances and learn much more about their incredible story. Films worth looking at include *Stormy Weather* starring jazz singer and actress Lena Horne and the 1992 arts and entertainment documentary about the life of the Nicholas Brothers entitled, *We Sing, We Dance.*

IN THEIR OWN WORDS...

We were tap-dancers, but we put more style into it, more bodywork, instead of just footwork.

Harold Nicholas

Fred Astaire (1899–1987)

On another branch of the jazz dance tree blooms Frederick Austerlitz, better known as Fred Astaire. His dance style, both as a choreographer and tap dancer, was very much influenced by ballroom dance, alongside the early jazz dance styles found in vaudeville. Astaire took inspiration from African-American tap dancers, such as Bojangles and John 'Bubbles' Sublett, in conjunction with the ballroom dance aesthetic of Vernon and Irene Castle. The influences of jazz rhythms, syncopation and the formal traditional stance and ballroom dance witnessed in the style of the Castles, formed the signature Astaire style and flair.

His new style of choreography was recognized as a new form of classic jazz dance that would take Hollywood films and the dance theatre to another level. Most significant was his pairing with dancer Ginger Rogers. Astaire and Rogers performed in nine films together, including *Top Hat* (1935), *Swing*

Image of Fred Astaire, studio publicity still for film *Daddy Long Legs* (1955).

Time (1936) and *Shall We Dance* (1937). Other dancing partners over his long career included Paulette Goddard, Rita Hayworth, Eleanor Powell, Audrey Hepburn and Cyd Charise.

Astaire innovated a new way of capturing dance on film, in that the camera moved with the dance, filming whole dance sequences without stopping. He worked closely with fellow choreographer Hermes Pan and together they created some of the most prolific tap dance and partner dance sequences in Hollywood film musicals. His formidable style and image as a dancer and choreographer brought him international acclaim and notoriety as a classic jazz dancer and choreographer of his generation.

IN THEIR OWN WORDS...

I have no desire to prove anything by my work. I have never used it as an outlet or as a means of expressing myself. I just dance.

Fred Astaire

Sammy Davis Jr (1925–90)

Sammy Davis Jr was a true Icon of jazz entertainment. A child star at the age of four years old, his journey as a young performer was instigated by his parents; in particular, his father and his adopted 'uncle' Will Marston, who already had a successful performing act. The young Sammy was added to the act and they became known as the Will Mastin Trio; later on the act became known as The Will Mastin Gang, Featuring Little Sammy.

As a tap dancer, actor, singer and comedian, his international acclaim took his career journey from the street to the vaudeville stage, to films, TV, concert halls, Broadway and Las Vegas, to performing for kings, queens and presidents to supporting the civil

Sammy Davis Jr performing on the television program *The Perry Como Show* (1966).

IN THEIR OWN WORDS...

You always have two choices: your commitment versus your fear.

Sammy Davies Jr

rights' plight in America. He also had his own American prime time TV show and an incredible recording career. He was recognized for his talent many times over with Emmy and Golden Globe nominations, to receiving a Grammy Lifetime Achievement Award.

It would be fair to say, Sammy Davis Jr has inspired and influenced many generations of performers after him. His relationship and mentorship to tap artists such as Gregory Hines and Savion Glover have been instrumental in passing on the baton of the tap dance traditions and roots of the jazz dance expression and aesthetic.

Women Waving the Flag for Tap Dance

Throughout much of its history, tap dance was often viewed as a male preserve. This in part was due to the producers of the times who invariably cast men to star in films and populist theatre productions. Although not always recognized,

Chorus line of female dancers in heels.

African-American female tap dancers were to be instrumental in choreographing and directing theatre shows. From as early as 1900, during the vaudeville era, African-American dancer Alice Whitman was to be hailed as the Queen of Tap. Along with her three equally talented sisters, the Whitman ladies founded their own performing production company, becoming the highest paid black performing artists on the vaudeville touring circuit. At the Cotton Club, and other small off-Broadway and travelling theatre shows, tap dance created and performed by women was to feature as the main dance attraction.

However, there is much written documentation and films worth reviewing and researching that offer further insight to the female tap dancers and dance artists, who set the standard as the leading ladies, achieving stardom and notoriety along the way in film and theatre dance and they include:

- Alice Whitman
- Anne Miller
- Diane Walker
- Eleanor Powell
- Florence Mills
- Ginger Rogers
- Harriet Brown
- Norma Miller
- Ruby Keeler
- Shirley Temple

THE BEAT GOES ON – THE NEXT GENERATION OF TAP VISIONARIES

Gregory Hines (1946–2003)

IN THEIR OWN WORDS...

I don't remember not dancing. When I realized I was alive and these were my parents, and I could walk and talk, I could dance.

Gregory Hines

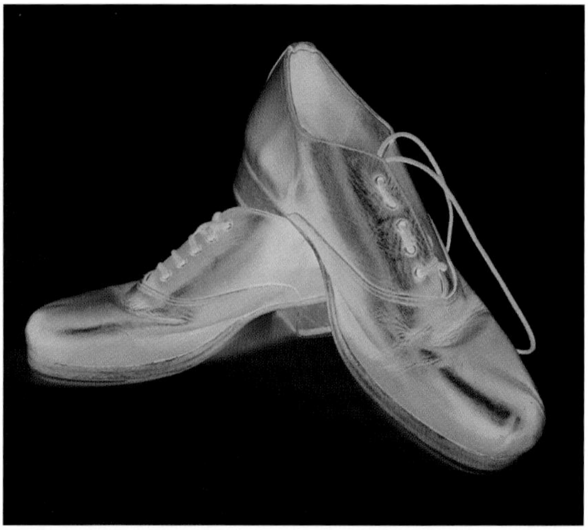

Silver tap shoes. BAFANA SOLOMAN MATEA

Due to other populist styles of dance entertainment, tap dance declined during the 1950s–1970s. However, during the 1980s, a new style of tap dance was brought into prominence by dancer, musician and actor Gregory Hines.

Hines was not only known as a dancer, but also a successful musician, singer, actor, choreographer and director. He had major influences and mentors in his life such as Sammy Davis Jr and Bill BoJangles, as well as many of the original hoofers. Inspired by past hoofers, he laid down a new incarnation for creative tap dance and this he shared through education, performances and his creative work. Hines' distinct dance and tap style was very much driven by the music, creating, as is the tradition of tap dance, a conversation between the tap sound, feet and the music. One of his unique attributes was that he used the music of the day (1980s) to create relevant artistic tap dance. His performance career is as extensive as it is varied. Prolific performances on Broadway gained him Tony Award nominations for the musicals *Comin' Uptown* (1979) and *Sophisticated Ladies* (1981), and a Drama Desk Award for *Jelly's Last Jam* (1992). Hines' film works included *Tap* (1989), his inspired television special *Gregory Hines: Tap Dance in America* and *White Nights* starring alongside classical dancer Mikhail Baryshnikov.

Savion Glover (1973–)

One of the most thrilling and inventive of tap dancers of our age has become the most instrumental influence for rhythm tap in the twenty-first century. Mentored and trained under the wings of a star list of names, including Gregory Hines, Sammy Davis Jr, Buster Brown and Jimmy Slyde, Glover was recognized as a tap dance prodigy and, at the age of ten, starred in the title role of the 1984 Broadway show *The Tap Dance Kid*. As a choreographer, he achieved a Tony Award for his creativity on the Broadway musical *Bring in da Noise, Bring in da Funk* (1996). He gained wider recognition when he provided all the tap dance creations for the movie franchise *Happy Feet*.

IN THEIR OWN WORDS...

I can produce any instrument, any sound that I can imagine; it may be percussive to the audience, but in my mind it may be a piano, a melody, or a tuba, or a harp, or a harmonica. My mission is to allow people to hear the dance in its purity and up against any other type of sound or music.

Savion Glover

More recently, Glover has developed and created a unique and distinct style from his own personal expression, which he calls free-form, hard core or power tapping. The emphasis and focus on accentuating and relating to rhythms and a groove, connecting tap steps and beats to the music rooted in hip-hop and funk music.

Tap Artists Making Their Own Beats

As we shuffle through the twenty-first century, the names below should also be mentioned and recognized for continuing the tap dance legacy. If you have not seen their work, visit their websites and YouTube channels and view them in action:

- Adam Garcia (Australia)
- Aleksandr Ostanin (Ukraine)
- Dien Perry (Australia)
- Daniel Borak (Switzerland)
- Junior Lanyian (UK)
- Kate Scanlan – Tap Attack (UK)
- Maude Arnold (USA)
- Michael Flatley (Irish/American)
- Michelle Dorrance (USA)
- Romain Rachline B. – RB Dance Company (France)
- Syncopated Ladies (USA)
- The Tap Twins – Sean and John Scott (USA)

Remy Martyn performing the tap dance *Caravan* from BOP Jazz Theatre production *Duke's Place*.

CHAPTER 3

THE ANTHOLOGY OF JAZZ MUSIC

THE BIRTH OF JAZZ MUSIC

From 1910 onwards, jazz had firmly established itself in the consciousness of American entertainment. As previously discussed, the early jazz music and jazz dance pioneers were inextricably linked. As the jazz idiom rose in popularity, so more and more venues started to appear that accommodated this new style of entertainment. These venues engaged famous bands of the day, bringing jazz music and jazz dance to the masses. The most famous of all jazz clubs, where dance was part of the main performance attraction, was the Cotton Club in New York.

The ascendancy of jazz music was further fuelled by the popularity of radio programmes and broadcasts that reached the masses by promoting the musicians, the bands, the jazz vocalists and jazz music as a whole. In turn, the jazz dancer and choreographer enjoyed unparalleled commercial success, reaching its height in the mid-1940s.

The jazz dancer and the jazz musician were very much cut from the same cloth. It was only when the music of bebop arrived on the musical landscape in the mid to late 1940s that jazz dance moved away from the innovative jazz music of the day. The dance gradually moved from a more improvised delivery and performance towards the more structured and technical creations that we see in musical theatre, concert theatre dance, film and television. The bebop revolution affected all of jazz. The music was no longer simply a type of populist entertainment. Bebop musicians went out of their way to disassociate themselves from popular culture. Consequently, the link between jazz dance and contemporary jazz music was broken. Both the music and the dance of jazz moved in separate directions for a while and sought different audiences and styles of creative expression.

OPPOSITE: **Dollie Henry.** HUGO GLENDINNING

Piano keys and jazz-playing hands.

Under the jazz music umbrella, there are countless styles of music to listen to and be engaged by, such as classic jazz standards, swing, big band, cool jazz, bebop, soul and rnb, funk, Latin jazz, fusion, orchestral jazz, world jazz, jazz hip-hop fusion and the many derivatives and experimental developments. Add to this an array of jazz musicians and vocalists, bandleaders and composers past and present who have and continue to share their musical talents, there is something for everyone to listen to and be inspired to dance and choreograph to.

Whatever the individual musical tastes and preferences, it is important to stay connected or, better still, re-connect to the rich source of musical branches that jazz music has produced and harvested. The jazz music collection from the early nineteenth century to our present day provides a vast canvas and rich musical sound-scape for jazz dance to continue developing in tune with its inherent musical partner.

What is clear in jazz music is syncretism – the blending together of cultural elements that previously existed separately. In its simplistic form, jazz music is an amalgam of differing styles that originate from the African, South American and European musical traditions.

- **African music** is often based on chant melody against complex syncopated beats. The voice sings the melody, whilst the drum holds the beat. The intricacy of the beat and the subdivision often makes for extremely complex and innovative polyrhythms. This syncopation and the placement of the beat are the driving forces of African music and, ultimately, the seed of jazz music.
- **South American music** is very much based on melodies, using a pentatonic scale. This fluid and harmonically 'simplistic' scale is very much part of the folklore music tradition of many nations.

Paul Jenkins and the BOP jazz quartet performing at Emma Cons Hall, London.

It can be heard throughout European cultures, including Germanic, Nordic, Celtic, alongside much of West African songs. Interestingly, the use of wind instruments in the South American tradition allowed for the manipulation or bending of individual notes, not unlike the 'blue notes' that are so often cited as an important feature of both blues and jazz music.

- **European music** has been analysed and critiqued throughout the last 500 years. Simply put, European music uses complex scales and harmony, and more orchestral textures.

TRACING THE JOURNEY OF JAZZ MUSIC

Congo Square

Clearly, jazz developed over many decades. In fact, it was not until the early twentieth century that the word 'jazz' was first used, initially a peculiar spelling of the word 'jass'. The first important historical location was Congo Square in New Orleans, Louisiana. It has been well documented that it was prohibitive, indeed, illegal to have slaves congregate in any numbers. However, in 1724 the French implemented Code Noir, which gave enslaved Africans the day off on Sundays. There were strict rules on slave activities, including religious worship, use of language and, in many regions, the use of drums was also illegal. A market was initially set up in Congo Square and, as almost a by-product, Africans slaves would sing, dance and play music. Much of the early rhythms were clearly derived from the African tradition, using the body and vocal improvisations. Eventually, musicians used percussion and string instruments – many almost identical to those used in Africa today.

Marching Bands

As an art form is shaped and developed it often reflects the cultural idiosyncrasies that are prevalent at that time. It is not surprising that the drum is a fundamental instrument in the development of jazz, as these instruments are easy to make.

Brass and wind instruments, which would eventually be the mainstay of the jazz band, were initially part of the marching band tradition, which was very much part of the musical culture of 1800s America. Trumpets, trombones and clarinets provided a forthright sound, punctuated by the rhythms of big bass drums.

These marching bands became part of daily life in New Orleans, not only as a celebration seen particularly at Mardi Gras, but also for funerals and general social gatherings. This tradition has continued to the present day and has greatly influenced the early days of jazz music.

Directly connected to Congo Square is the music. Marching bands were always accompanied by dance that reflected in movement the emotional direction of the music. In funeral processions, the music and dance followed a formulaic pattern. Moving to the burial, the dance and music would be slow and mournful, reflecting the emotion of the moment. After burial the music would take a distinct turn and play fast, up-beat syncopated music and the dance constantly reflected this sound. A tradition that continues today in New Orleans

Minstrelsy

The movement of music and dance artists to enlighten and entertain is a tradition that goes back many hundreds of years. We only need to think of medieval minstrels in the West and the African tradition of griots to exemplify this. The beginnings of jazz music and dance followed a similar directional path, and travelling shows were very much part of the entertaining fabric from the 1800s. Black entertainers would provide a variety of musical and dance styles and movement that proved extremely popular. These performances eventually developed into minstrel shows.

Towards the end of the nineteenth century, New Orleans boasted many musicians, ensembles and bands, who were moving towards the sound eventually recognized as jazz. One of the first musical jazz styles to gain popularity was ragtime – a style of jazz music that was to greatly influence early jazz musicians and jazz dance.

***The Entertainer* sheet music cover, by Scott Joplin.**

In the Beginning There Was 'Ragtime'

Towards the end of the nineteenth century, ragtime was developed almost single-handedly by one of the first jazz innovators, Scott Joplin. Ragtime was an extremely syncopated style of music that was fast and lively, and perfect for dancing. This music was incorporated in the music of marching bands who would combine the structure of marches with black songs and dances, such as the cakewalk.

It was the development of music for the piano that greatly popularized this style of jazz music, coupled with the explosion of sales of the upright piano. Interestingly, this music gave very little space for improvisation, being highly stylized and structured. This in turn enabled ragtime to be easily translated into both sheet music and piano rolls, so increasing its popularity across America.

The Ragtime Sound

The music is heavily syncopated and tightly structured. It was primarily performed on the piano. The syncopation was generally in the treble part with accompaniment provided by the left hand. There was an element of stride where the single bass note is quickly followed by chords for harmony. The more important compositions were *Maple Leaf Rag*, *The Cakewalk* and *Harlem Rag*.

RAGTIME PIONEERS

- Scott Joplin
- Fats Waller
- Eubie Blake
- Jelly Roll Morton
- William 'the Lion' Smith
- James P. Johnson

New Orleans' Traditional Jazz

In the early twentieth century, the city of New Orleans, the area considered to be responsible for the birth of jazz, was a melting pot of peoples and cultures. Certainly, much of the dancing and drumming was rooted in the African tradition, and the continuing development of the up-tempo and syncopated ragtime profoundly influenced the early jazz pioneers.

Marching bands had begun to influence New Orleans' music, in terms of musical forms and types of instruments, mainly brass and wind instruments. The night-life of New Orleans provided a home for the beginnings of jazz. Many musicians were based in the red-light district of New Orleans, known as Storyville. Eventually, this music become known as hot jazz as it incorporated the fast and syncopated rhythms of ragtime, but scored for a larger ensemble, often comprising of trumpets, trombones, saxophones, clarinets, banjos, drums and bass and the tuba.

Unlike ragtime, there was much emphasis on improvisation and, more often, the compositions were learnt aurally and never written down. Once established, New Orleans' jazz was to influence the entire jazz canon and some of the most important pioneers of jazz music resided in New Orleans. Many early jazz musicians credited Buddy Bolden

Louis Armstrong (1955).

THE FIRST JAZZ PIONEERS

- Louis Armstrong
- Buddy Bolden
- Kid Ory
- King Oliver
- Sidney Bechet

and the members of his band with being the originators of jazz.

The Oliver–Ory band was the first great jazz group and along with Kid Ory and King Oliver the band also included Louis Armstrong. Louis Armstrong was to become the first superstar of jazz; he was one of the greatest jazz musicians of all time and a true innovator.

Chicago Jazz – a New Jazz Sound Emerges

The music of jazz was becoming more and more popular throughout the USA as the country's infrastructure developed, particularly after the official closing of the district of Storyville, New Orleans, in 1927. Many jazz musicians began migrating north, first to Chicago and, eventually, to New York.

Alongside and throughout the first two decades of the twentieth century, sound recording and broadcast developed rapidly, so that by the 1920s, gramophone records and daily broadcasts were the norm. This allowed for the rapid development of the jazz sound.

As the music developed, the sound of jazz became instantly recognizable. The pulse of the music emanated from the drums and bass instruments. The harmony parts were filled by piano or banjo, and the lead lines by trumpet, clarinet and trombone. The sound generated was exciting, challenging, syncopated and, above all, made for dancing.

PIONEERS OF THE NEW JAZZ SOUND

- Bix Beiderbeck
- Clarence Williams
- Freddie Keppard

Early Swing Music

As the audience of jazz began to broaden due to records, so did the musicians. From New Orleans, through to Chicago on to New York by the end of the 1920s, the music had infiltrated all parts of America and had begun to exert its influence on popular culture world-wide. One of the most important early jazz recordings came from Louis Armstrong and his *Hot 5* and *Hot 7* sessions. These recordings, in 1925 and 1928, radically altered jazz's focus; instead of collective playing, Armstrong's innovative instrumental and vocal performances redefined jazz. The emphasis was now on individual improvisations. Armstrong introduced scat singing and with his virtuoso trumpet solo, he established the jazz stop time technique.

The Jazz Sound

As jazz celebrated the individual creative, so the styles and sounds of early jazz continued to be augmented and developed. By the 1920s, the music had very much moved 'indoors' and became central to popular entertainment. Drummers added more drums and cymbals to their kit. The bass was the sound that underpinned all jazz and was now being performed by a plucked acoustic bass. The piano had become the dominant harmony instrument. The trumpet still remained king of all lead instruments, but the recently invented saxophone was rising in prominence and about to take a lead role in the sound of jazz.

Many important musicians rose to prominence through the late 1920s and 1930s. These pioneers were to play an enormous role in the development and movement of jazz:

- Lester Young
- Ben Webster
- Coleman Hawkins
- Paul Whiteman
- Cab Calloway
- Tommy Dorsey
- Chick Webb
- Jimmie Lanceford

The Swing Sound

The early swing sound was mainly composed of, and generally consisted of, small repeated phrases or riffs that moved between the instruments of the ensemble. As the style evolved, more contrapuntal ideas developed, although always over an intense moving rhythm.

Duke Ellington Big Band, Munich (1963). HANS BERNHARD

The placement of the beat by both singled line instruments and members of the rhythm section was highly important and enabled a rhythmic intensity that characterizes jazz swing music.

Improvisation was given a much more featured role, and soloists would play while the rest of the band, aside from the rhythm section, dropped out or played background riffs. This enabled the music to be constantly evolving and challenging. The soloist attempted, in each improvised solo, to express not only their individual musical approach, but also technical proficiency on the instruments. The swing era enabled many innovative and pioneering instrumentalists to develop unique jazz voices that reflected the great variety and diversity of instrumental sound.

The Rise of the Big Band

The music of the swing era was slowly woven into the entertainment fabric of America. Dance halls and theatres presented many great jazz bands, eventually leading to the formation of swing big bands. Before the 1930s, small ensembles, usually consisting of only a trumpet, trombone, clarinet, tuba or bass, banjo or piano, and drums, performed jazz, and parts were often improvised. The big bands of swing music featured larger sections of three or four trumpeters, three or four trombonists, five saxophonists, a piano, a bassist, a guitarist and a drummer, generating enough power and energy to fill a large performance space and often used for the associated style of jazz dance.

Duke Ellington is often considered to be the greatest jazz composer of all time. Many of his compositions are recognized today as jazz standards, such as *It Don't Mean a Thing*, *Take the A Train* and *Sophisticated Lady*. He also composed longer works, including *Black and Tan Fantasy*, *New Orleans Suite* and *Black*, *Brown and Beige*. And he was no stranger to creating scores for concert theatre dance and musical theatre.

IN THEIR OWN WORDS...

Critics have their purposes, and they're supposed to do what they do, but sometimes they get a little carried away with what they think someone should have done, rather than concerning themselves with what they did.

Duke Ellington

THE SWING JAZZ PIONEERS

- Duke Ellington
- Count Basie
- Fletcher Henderson
- Benny Goodman
- Earl Hines
- Glenn Miller
- Tommy Dorsey

After forming small jazz ensembles in his native Washington, Duke Ellington and his fame spread nationwide when his orchestra became the house band at the famous Cotton Club in Harlem. Following his engagement at the Cotton Club, Ellington continued to lead his orchestra right up until his death in 1974. His orchestra became an extension of his creative musical output, creating a unique jazz sound.

Many of his musicians played in Ellington's orchestra for decades and were often woven intrinsically into the Ellington sound: Johnny Hodges, Ben Webster and Clarke Terry, to name a few. Although his music was composed, it gave great freedom to the improvisers in the ensemble. Ellington has left an indelible mark on the music and history of jazz music.

The Rise of the Jazz Singer

As microphone technology improved, singers began to be essential to the success of any big band. Bessie Smith, Mahalia Jackson, Billie Holiday, Ella Fitzgerald, Sarah Vaughan and Louis Armstrong, all became singing sensations. Band leader Tommy Dorsey hired the young Frank Sinatra who went on to dominate this new form of 'popular jazz' along-

Billie Holiday at the Downbeat Club, New York. *c.* February 1947.

WILLIAM P. GOTTLIE.

side Nat King Cole, Tony Bennett, Billie Eckstine, Dina Washington, Betty Carter, Nancy Wilson and Sammy Davis Jr.

The jazz vocalist continues to be popular today, with many on both sides of the Atlantic achieving international recognition, including Dianne Reeves, Dee Dee Bridgewater, Diana Krall, Harry Connick Jr, Michael Bublé, Nora Jones, Dame Cleo Laine, Claire Martin OBE, Stacey Kent, Jamie Cullum and, more currently, Gregory Porter and Esperanza Spalding.

IN THEIR OWN WORDS...

I think the idea is now for blacks to write about the history of our music. It's time for that, because whites have been doing it all the time. It's time for us to do it ourselves and tell it like it is.

Dizzy Gillespie

The Bebop Revolution

In the 1940s, a revolution in the development and direction of jazz occurred. Throughout the previous forty years, jazz music had been primarily for popular entertainment. However, this was all set to change at Minton's Playhouse in New York, where a new and exciting jazz style was being formed. The driving energy behind this new style, which became known as bebop, were Charlie Parker and Dizzy Gillespie. These two musical giants were to change the music forever, from populist entertainment to high art.

The Bebop Sound

In juxtaposition to the sound of the big band, the bebop sound was created through small groups, normally saxophone, trumpet and rhythm section. Improvisation was the main focus and often solos would last four or five minutes, bearing little reference to the melody.

In turn, the melodies were fast and complicated, and new modern harmonic approaches were heard. The rhythm section often displaced the beat with fast, syncopated rhythms that made it impossible to dance to. Virtuoso playing was the order of the day and play.

- **Charlie Parker** is simply one of the greatest saxophonists of all time. His approach to improvisations and, in particular, his harmonic development and instrumental virtuosity are without parallel. His recordings are his legacy, which are full of imagination, excitement and musical beauty.

- **Dizzy Gillespie**, like Parker, was an instrumental virtuoso. His blistering trumpet solos were the sound of bebop. His compositions and approaches to improvisation are full of the bebop sound. He was also instrumental in bringing Cuban rhythm to jazz to create a style in jazz known as Afro-Cuban. His composition *Manteca* is a perfect example.

Dizzy Gillespie (1955). This work is from the Carl Van Vechten photographs collection at the Library of Congress.

THE BEBOP PIONEERS

- Thelonious Monk
- Max Roach
- Kenny Clarke
- Bud Powell
- J.J. Johnson
- Clifford Brown
- Art Tatum
- Ray Brown

Cool Jazz

In the 1950s, a new style of jazz emerged that was the opposite of bebop. The emphasis was placed back on to the ensemble sound and the improvised solos were more reflective and less frantic. The harmony became less complex and reverted back to sixteenth-century music with the use of modes. Large ensembles and orchestrations developed the approach further, from which the sound of cool jazz music emerged.

Miles Davis is one of the most influential jazz musicians and composers of the time. He is often credited with changing the direction of jazz many times over. He led and brought together some of the greatest jazz groups and ensembles for live and recorded performances. Having played with the great saxophonist Charlie Parker, who was also part of the bebop revolution, Davis realized that a different approach to jazz was needed and along with composer Gill Evans, they created a style of music that is now known as cool jazz.

As early as 1949–50, they had recorded *The Birth of the Cool*, which revolutionized jazz composition and arrangement. This was followed by the recordings and albums of *Miles Ahead*, *Porgy and Bess* and *Sketches of Spain*, an orchestral jazz composition inspired by Rodrigo's classical guitar concerto. However, his greatest cool album was the seminal *Kind of Blue*. Following his cool period, Miles continued to develop and moved into progressive jazz and jazz fusion. Miles Davis is possibly one of the most influential jazz musicians of all time.

THE COOL JAZZ PIONEERS

Both in the East and West of America cool jazz was the sound of the 1950s. A number of musicians rose to prominence and adapted the cool approach to their style of playing. Some of the pioneers include:

- Chet Baker
- Gerry Mulligan
- John Lewis
- Dave Brubeck
- Bill Evans
- Stan Getz

IN THEIR OWN WORDS...

I'm always thinking about creating. My future starts when I wake up every morning. Every day I find something creative to do with my life.

Miles Davies

Following bebop, the influence of jazz on populist dance became even more blurred. As the cool jazz style was orchestral and reflective, the musical palate was more conducive to artistic and concert theatre dance. However, popular styles of music were beginning to take hold and jazz dance moved back to its entertaining roots, where the jazz style was becoming less influential. The stage, screen and television were to be the jazz dancers' 'new' home.

Hard Bop

The jazz style had continued to develop and evolve, and new derivative styles and movements gathered in pace to its peak in the 1970s.

Hard bop was the first style to be directly influenced by bebop. The music had a more compulsive rhythmic drive. The ensemble playing was tighter and funkier. The music was also influenced by rnb, blues and gospel, and looked to appeal to a wider audience.

In some ways, it was a reaction to cool jazz, which was partly influenced by European classical music.

Miles Davis, Nice Jazz Festival (1989).
OLIVER NUROCK

HARD BOP PIONEERS

Through hard bop, many musicians gained international fame. The new generation was influenced by many different musical styles, which they incorporated in to their own style. The result was great diversity in execution. Some important musicians include:

- Art Blakey
- Freddie Hubbard
- Sonny Rollins
- Art Farmer
- Wes Montgomery

Hard bop is characterized by its focus on African-American musical styles. It also led directly to a more riff-style of playing, which eventually developed into funk music.

Horace Silver, along with Art Blakey, were the front-runners of hard bop, forming the band the Jazz Messengers. But it was Horace Silver, with his funkier, blues-tinged piano-playing that impacted the most on this new style and greatly influenced mainstream contemporary jazz music. His compositions are still played today and the seminal *Song for My Father* is a great example of the hard bop style.

Jazz music manuscript.

OTHER FREE JAZZ MUSICIANS

In the 1950s, Coleman worked with a select group of musicians who shared his view on this style of jazz:

- Ornette Coleman
- Don Cherry
- Billie Higgins
- Charlie Haden
- Eric Dolphy
- John Coltrane

Free Jazz

As jazz music became more harmonically and rhythmically diverse, it was inevitable that the move to an unstructured and a more 'freer' style of playing would emerge. Of all jazz music styles, free jazz is the most challenging, as it places great demands on both the performer and the listener.

It was very much inspired by a Western harmonic approach and the avant-garde. When first heard in the late 1950s, it was called 'anti-jazz'. However, this almost intellectual approach to improvisation was its natural progression; the ability to play in the moment, with no harmonic and structural barriers, was incredibly liberating musically.

Despite its initial detractors, this style of music went on to inspire a whole new generation of musicians. Free jazz as an entertainment was very much in question; free jazz to dance to, absolutely not.

Although Lennie Tristano recorded the first free jazz album in 1949, it was Ornette Coleman who was to become the leading light of the new movement when, in 1958, he released *Something Else*. This was followed the next year with the seminal album *The Shape of Jazz to Come*. His music was revolutionary, free from all conformity and, in some way, the essence of jazz.

Jazz Fusion

Through the late 1960s and early 1970s there was a great amalgam of different sounds and styles in music. In particular, some jazz musicians moved to incorporate electronic instruments and amplification into their music. Jazz fusion sought to embrace these instrumental changes along with mixing funk, rnb and rock elements. The resulting sound was often large, amplified and loud. Improvisation was still at the forefront of the music, although the rhythms owed more to the rock back-beat than swing.

One early pioneer was Miles Davis, who had been experimenting with electronic instruments with his band towards the end of the 1960s. It is widely accepted that his album *Bitches Brew* (1969) was the first influential jazz fusion album. At the time, his band included musicians who were to become important players in this new style: Joe Zawinul, Chick Corea, John Mclauglin and Lenny White.

Weather Report

Weather Report was one of the most influential of all jazz fusion bands. They had incredible commercial success, including hit singles. The group was co-led by Joe Zawinul and Wayne Shorter, and included the remarkable electric bass player, Jaco Pastorius.

Despite commercial success, the music was incredibly complex and its sound was the masterful blending of early synthesizers and saxophone with complex rhythmic grooves. *Heavy Weather* (1977) and *Weather Report* (1982) were their most successful albums.

Mahavishnu Orchestra

The Mahavishnu Orchestra was formed by John Mclaughlin and was much more rock-oriented. With Billy Cobham on drums, the explosive rhythm propelled this virtuosic music. Strongly influenced by eastern mysticism, the jazz orchestra quickly gained wide popularity and broke new boundaries in jazz fusion with albums like *The Inner Mountain Flame* (1971) and *Birds of Fire* (1972).

OTHER FUSION GROUPS

- Return to Forever
- Headhunters
- Blood, Sweat and Tears

Contemporary Jazz Fusion

Over the last thirty years, jazz has witnessed enormous change in its sound and approach. A number of important musicians and groups use contemporary sounds and structures fused with more traditional approaches. Drum loops might be incorporated alongside acoustic drums, while the saxophone would be blended with synthesizer sounds. EWI or electronic wind sound are used by saxophone and trumpet players to access computer sounds.

Improvisation is still an important part of the music and, more often, advanced harmony forms the basis of the compositions.

Pioneers of Contemporary Jazz Fusion

Jazz ensembles, such as Steps Ahead, lead by vibraphonist Mike Mainieri, and the Yellow Jackets, used advanced harmonic progressions and a combination of acoustic and synthesized sounds, fusing contemporary jazz harmony with complex and shifting rhythmic intensity with exciting improvisations.

The Pat Metheny Group was inspired by one of the most influential jazz guitarists of the last thirty years, Pat Metheny. He performs across a variety of styles and forms, from the free jazz of Ornette Coleman to the pop music of David Bowie. However, he is best known for his group co-led with pianist Lyle Mays. Much is often a kaleidoscope of sound and emotion, but always underpinned by amazingly crafted improvisations by both Metheny and Mays. Some of the more popular albums are *Travels*, *First Circle*, *Still Life Talking* and *Imaginary Day*.

Smooth Jazz

Following on from the jazz fusion genre, jazz musicians sought to collaborate across differing musical styles. Consequently, throughout the 1980s, new jazz styles emerged, such as acid jazz, soul jazz, nu-jazz and jazz-rap. These more popular jazz styles were collected under the umbrella of smooth jazz.

The Sound of Smooth Jazz

As music technology developed, so the use of modern timbres became incorporated in the sound of smooth jazz, such as drum loops, synthesizer sounds and electronic wind instruments. The saxophone rose to prominence as the sound of early smooth jazz. The guitar also became a popular lead instrument, with its array of distinctive and commercial sounds. Improvisation took a backward seat as populist grooves and funky horn riffs punctuated the genre.

CONNECTING TO THE BEAT OF JAZZ MUSIC IN THE TWENTY-FIRST CENTURY

Without a doubt, jazz was the most influential art form of the twentieth century. It has conquered all areas of the globe, shaping, changing amalgamating and producing a myriad of sounds and movements. All musical genres have been approached and fused, creating new and original sounds and compositions.

At its heart, jazz music is still the genius of the improvising musician. The art form of jazz cannot exist without the creative performers and innovators who shape and develop individual sounds and compositions, as they themselves experience and connect with their own personal and creative lives.

The Future Sound of Jazz Music

As the art form continues to develop and diversify, we have an ever-increasing array of musical subgenres that are influenced by jazz, such as orchestral jazz, rap jazz, world jazz, hip-hop jazz, acoustic jazz, acid jazz, soul jazz, European jazz, contemporary jazz, Latin jazz and Brazilian jazz.

The inevitable consequences of an open and free art form are its musical and cultural diversifications. Thankfully jazz has lived through over a hundred years of recordings. This has allowed us to capture, in recorded form, all the great movements of jazz from its first recording in 1927 to its present-day streaming.

As with all living and breathing art forms, the best thing any dancer or musician can do is continue to search, to make a conscience effort to listen, to appreciate and to enjoy. The benefits are plentiful and can only inform and inspire our own development, musically and artistically.

Paul Jenkins and his trumpet.

SIMON RICHARDSON

CHAPTER 4

A NEW ERA – MODERN JAZZ DANCE

THE TRANSITION OF AUTHENTIC JAZZ INTO MODERN JAZZ DANCE

Throughout the first part of the twentieth century there was an exponential development of jazz dance. The success of the jazz idiom became so well established in America that its influence was seen across all forms of entertainment.

Jazz began to hit a meteoric rise during the 1920s, which became known as 'The Jazz Age', continuing its stride through the 1930s and rising to a peak in the 1940s. Consequently, all types of entertainment displayed the jazz influence, from the travelling shows, minstrelsy, vaudeville into musical theatre, films and later television.

The same movement was also happening to jazz music through the development of gramophones and the radio. Jazz music attracted unprecedented success as it was listened to throughout America and the rest of the world. As jazz music and jazz dance were still intrinsically linked, both displayed rapid artistic growth and increasing creative diversity, and also separation moving through the following decades.

It is important to note that at this time in America the only form of dance considered 'artistic' was classical dance. All other dance forms were viewed as populist or social entertainment. Therefore, there was little need to classify jazz dance as a technique aside from identifying the more popular jazz dance styles of the time; for example, the Charleston, lindy-hop, Jitterbug, swing dance. For jazz dance this presented a problem, as there was no effective way to identify the individual jazz dance exponents, aside from grouping them all under the same 'jazz dance' umbrella.

OPPOSITE: **Dollie Henry and David Olton. Commissioned drawing by artist and sculptor Brenda Naylor.**

Dancers in New Yorker Dance Shoes.

After World War II, dance entertainment was moving rapidly into film. Many dancers and choreographers were developing impressive careers across all arts' platforms and, therefore, there was the need for a jazz dance vocabulary to instruct the dancers. Over time, dance choreographer's and their personal dance styles and techniques became recognizable, with many laying their individual methods and practice, so setting a standard for jazz dance techniques, through movement, steps and stylistic interpretations, which are still used to represent jazz dance today.

As the jazz expression moved through the 1940s, a number of jazz choreographers, who are mentioned later, began seeking a deeper depth of artistry and a more meaningful creative outcome to their dance creations, developing their particular jazz style and technique into standards for teaching in education and artistic company settings. Jazz dance was to develop and move in very different directions, which in turn was to inspire a whole generation of jazz dancer and jazz creatives. This is no surprise, as it reflects the basic idiomatic premise of jazz, in that it stems from an individual's creative response and relationship to the jazz expression, the aesthetic and the music.

The Personalities of Modern Jazz Dance

Although there was little detail in the codification of jazz dance, a new dance term emerged that sought to more easily classify and identify varying dance forms – that of modern dance. On one hand, the term modern dance helped to separate the techniques and creative outcomes between classical dance and other developing dance forms outside of ballet. On the other hand, it grouped together many

Nadia Strahan, Paul Bailey, David Olton performing in *Dizzy Heights*, BOP Jazz Theatre.

differing choreographers who expressed many differing styles and techniques. Modern dance is quintessentially a fusion between jazz dance and classical/contemporary dance. It was under the umbrella of modern dance that the seed of artistic jazz dance and jazz theatre was born. Interestingly, moving through the modern dance era was no longer appropriate to describe the works of choreographers outside of the jazz dance idiom. A new term, that of contemporary dance, the antithesis of ballet, became a new line of creative dance. In the UK throughout the 1970s and 1980s, the term modern dance was used to describe jazz dance and set the tone for syllabus dance examinations within many dancing schools and performing arts' colleges.

Delving deeper into the complexities of the term modern dance, with an understanding of the history and lineage of the jazz dance idiom, we can begin to identify the jazz aesthetic and the emerging derivatives of jazz dance. This is primarily through the works of individual choreographers and jazz dance practitioners who had developed a definable style and technique.

It is fair to say that from the 1930s and into the 1940s modern dance became a myriad of styles and techniques, and modern jazz dance was no different. However, for simplicity, and in order to acknowledge the wide spectrum of practices within the jazz dance idiom, we will categorize choreographers of this period and their work under two distinct headings:

- **Show-jazz dance** aligned to the populistic and commercial performance and entertainment of musical theatre, film and television.
- **Concert-jazz dance** aligned to the artistic and creative development of narrative jazz dance theatre, often realized within a dance company or dance group setting.

Both are part of the same branch, but differ in their theatrical presentation, creative approaches, musical interpretations and, fundamentally, the delivery and practice of the jazz dance aesthetic and expression.

SHOW DANCE AND ALL THAT JAZZ

Possibly the most influential form of populist stage entertainment over the last fifty-plus years has been musical theatre. The scope of this book is to express an overview of the journey of jazz dance, of which musical theatre plays a vital role. Although very much ensconced in commercial popularity, musical theatre has provided a platform for many dancers and choreographers to introduce their unique style and interpretation of jazz dance, so influencing and shaping musical theatre dance.

When considering musical theatre, one of the most amazing reflections is the myriad of individual styles and dance techniques there are. For example, consider the vaudeville and burlesque jazz dance influences and the physical stylistic expression of Bob Fosse, to that of the classically inspired and motivated jazz dance creations of Jerome Robbins. Both differ in their dance styles and technique, but both are considered icons of musical theatre jazz dance.

The Black and White of it

It is important to acknowledge that the commerciality of musical theatre did affect the choice of choreographers who worked within the genre. Throughout much of the twentieth century, there was still a clear racial divide throughout American society that extended to the arts. Black creatives (although more accepted as performers) were denied the open opportunity to work on Broadway or film and early television as creative choreographers, writers and directors. Therefore, it is not surprising that many of the early recognizable pioneers of the modern musical theatre were white.

Although black creatives were originating musical theatre productions and created work of a jazz disposition that reflected the African-American experience, these shows were never given the platform or opportunity to succeed. However, as jazz was the inclusive art form of the time, many white choreographers were greatly influenced by the black jazz tradition and adopted many of the styles and techniques into their own work. For many years this appropriation of the African-American artistic tradition was not acknowledged and, understandably, was the cause of much anger and frustration within the black artistic community. Thankfully, we are slowly moving into a position where the creative work of the early jazz pioneers and latter-day icons are appropriately recognized and championed for the enormous contribution that they had on the shaping of musical theatre and artistic concert dance.

It is beyond the remit of this book but it should be noted that much of what is considered popular music and dance culture can find its origins in the streets of the urban environment. The jazz dance trajectory was on a similar path of evolution that was shaped from the early authentic (vernacular) jazz dances of minstrelsy and steaming through to vaudeville. Then came the advent of jazz dance in film, on Broadway and, later, as part of the MTV generation. What is very clear throughout history is that jazz dance is the organic expression that links directly to black performers throughout the nineteenth century.

There are many books on the history of musical theatre. As this is a guide book, it concentrates on the choreographers whose stylistic approaches and theatrical creative outcomes have set the standard image and style for the jazz dance form in musical theatre.

Influential Musical Theatre Jazz Choreographers

Jack Cole (1911–74)

The name Jack Cole is often recalled as the 'father of modern theatre jazz'. Cole came from a contemporary and classical dance background and honed his craft as a company dancer with Ruth St. Denis and Ted Shawn. His style developed through the fusing of modern dance techniques, jazz and other ethnic dances. His style and technique was said to require his dancers to attain the high technical dance ability found in classical dance, whilst keeping the energy and influences of jazz and world dance.

The Cole dance style was very grounded to the floor and the use of 'plié' shows to be a driving force behind his powerful and controlled choreography. His career as a choreographer and director straddled Broadway shows, night clubs, film and TV. He was one of the early jazz practitioners who set up his own dance classes, providing professional and student dancers with his specific jazz style and technique in preparation for a professional career in dance theatre.

Musicals and films Cole has choreographed and/or directed include *Kismet*, *A Funny Thing Happened on the Way to the Forum*, *Jamaica*, *Man of La Mancha*, *The Merry Widow*, *Gentlemen Prefer Blondes*, *There's No Business Like Show Business* and *Some Like It Hot*. Jack Cole was to be a great influence on future choreographers Bob Fosse and Jerome Robbins, star dancers like Gwen Verdon, teachers such as Matt Mattox, notwithstanding inspiring many more dancers and choreographers at this time of change in jazz dance in the 1940s and 1950s.

Michael Kidd (1915–2007)

Kidd started his career as a ballet dancer rising to soloist of ballet theatre (American Ballet Theatre), where he was greatly influenced by Jerome Robbins, as he performed in Robbins' famous work *Fancy Free*. His first great success was with the iconic film musical *Guys and Dolls*, where he established his style in the jazz tradition. He went on to choreograph *Seven Brides for Seven Brothers* and the film version of *Hello Dolly* with Barbra Streisand. His individual style was very much in tune with the jazz tradition, expressing reality through the dance and the importance of dance characterization, through movement and dance that stemmed from real life expression or as he has noted 'naturalistic movement'.

Jerome Robbins (1918–98)

Robbins was the master of combining both a career in musical theatre and ballet. Robbins was able to fuse his incredible artistry of classical dance, which provided a technical and lyrical quality, and his inspired perception of jazz dance, which gave the dynamics and energy to his choreography.

His creativity and style of theatre direction pushed the musical theatre dance format to a completely new level. His great works still thrill today. *West Side Story* has stood the test of time, alongside his other great musical triumphs: *The King and I*, *Fiddler on the Roof*, *Gypsy* and *Funny Girl*. Robbins was a dance director and choreographic genius, and one of the finest innovators of creative musical theatre in the twentieth century.

Bob Fosse (1927–87)

Anyone who has ever taken jazz dance as a main subject, either academically or practically, will know the name Bob Fosse. To this day, in our dance education and performing world, the name of Fosse is held up as one of the long-lasting influences of jazz dance on stage and on screen.

Fosse is amongst the most important choreographers of the twentieth century. Although his career had many different facets, he was very much inspired by the jazz music tradition, vaudeville theatre and burlesque shows. These influences all played out in his creative works. However, his work is greatly influenced by his own physical abilities.

It is well known that Fosse had a physical deformity that affected his posture and legs. Therefore, it is not surprising that his work is often angular, physically constrained and not that expansive. Yet like all creative geniuses, he turned these afflictions into his own jazz dance language.

His choreographic style and narrative generally put the emphasis on female characters, with story lines that gave the female narrative a provocative and, at times, an aggressive edge. To witness this, you only have to see his creative dance styles in his musicals, *Chicago*, *Cabaret* and *Sweet Charity*.

Dancer Alex Frei captures a stylistic dance pose illustrating the jazz style of Bob Fosse.

TATJANA JENTSCH

IN THEIR OWN WORDS...

Don't dance for the audience, dance for yourself.

Bob Fosse

Without a doubt, Fosse created a unique jazz dance style. He used isolations as a form of dance movement, hip punches, head rolls and rib isolations. Fosse easily created distorted movements that blended so effortlessly with his style of dance choreography to exciting and ground-breaking effect, all a throwback to his burlesque days. Think of black dance attire and fishnet tights, the bowler hat, walking canes and white gloves – this is the stylistic influence of Fosse. Interestingly, this is the exact attire and prop (cane) that black performers used in the minstrel/vaudeville shows as part of the cakewalk.

As an innovator, director and choreographer of stage and screen, Fosse was able to elevate jazz dance in musical theatre with his iconic, often sexy, but always feminine style. His works are represented and produced over and over again. His style and technique continue to inspire some of today's performing artists and have even influenced music videos, such as *Single Ladies*, performed by rnb singer/performer Beyoncé and her dancers.

Gene Kelly (1912–96)

Kelly followed on from the dance film tradition set by Fred Astaire. Kelly developed his technique to become one of the most recognized and innovative film and musical performers of all time. He started his Broadway dance career with Cole Porter's *Leave Me Alone*, but attracted recognition playing the lead in *Pal Joey* with choreography by Robert Altman. He moved quickly into film with his first film musical *For Me and My Gal*. He began his choreographic journey in film with the part-animated *Anchors Away*, followed by a series of hit film musicals that continue in popularity today, through musical stage productions *On the Town*, *The Pirate*, *An America in Paris*, *Singing in The Rain* and *Invitation to Dance*.

His choreography was very much influenced by his particular dance style. His style was compact and powerful in appearance and physical display. This resulted in giving his jazz dance style a real sense of masculine athleticism and energy. As a jazz artist, Kelly looked at all forms of dance and incorporated many differing styles into his creative works, not only jazz and classical, but also contemporary and folk dance, in particular, Irish clog dancing.

As a performer, on the big screen and as a choreographer of an era, Kelly was the master of creating memorable dance sequences in film, which still stand the test of time. He created a vision for jazz dance that influenced many male dancers and choreographers after him.

IN THEIR OWN WORDS...

I wanted to do new things with dance, adapt it to the motion picture medium.

Gene Kelly

These are the obvious recognized names of choreographers synonymous with musical theatre and film. On the other side, there are also many other names that have not always been represented or highlighted in the same infamous way. Many have been able to cross both the artistic and commercial divide to accentuate their own creative jazz expression beyond the musical theatre format.

Michael Bennett (1943–87)

A dancer, choreographer, theatre director and writer, Bennett made a big impact on the Broadway theatre. He began his dance career as a teenager on the touring production of *West Side Story.* Early choreographic work led to two Sondheim productions, *Company* and *Follies*. Bennett will be best remembered for the musical *Chorus Line*, based on the personal and individual stories of a chorus line of dancers. As a choreographer and director, he placed great artistic importance of characterization in dance, to show the personality of the dancer, either perceived or real, evident in performance. His other important work is *Dreamgirls*, which he directed and co-choreographed with African-American choreographer Michael Peters. The production is very much influenced by black culture and creative influences that came with the 1960s black dance movement and pop music.

Michael Bennett was the recipient of seven Tony Awards and additional theatre awards for direction and choreography for his Broadway shows. His other Broadway work includes *Follies*, *Company* and *Promises Promises*.

George Faison (1945–)

For more than forty years, Faison has been a force in concert dance and musical theatre, as well as film, video, television commercials and trade shows. Like all prolific jazz artists, his jazz style amalgamates and fuses modern jazz and contemporary dance trends with black American dance theatre.

In the late 1960s, he rose to prominence as an Alvin Ailey dancer, later choreographing works for the company, including *Suite Otis*. On leaving Ailey, he formed his concert dance company, the George Faison Universal Dance Experience, fusing jazz, contemporary and commercial dance styles.

Faison made his choreographic debut on Broadway with *Don't Bother Me, I Can't Cope* (1972). In 1974, he choreographed *The Wiz*, the successful all-black musical retelling of *The Wizard of Oz*, winning a Tony Award for choreography, the first for an African-American in that category. He has choreographed and directed more than thirty plays and musicals, including, on Broadway, *Via Galactica* (1973) and *1600 Pennsylvania Avenue* (1976), and the Radio City Music Hall production of *Porgy and Bess* (1983) and *Sing, Mahalia, Sing* (1985). He has worked extensively in television and, in 1989, he conceived and produced the television special *Cosby Salutes Ailey* for the 30th anniversary of the Alvin Ailey American Dance Theater. He won an Emmy Award for his choreography of the HBO special *The Josephine Baker Story* (1991). Moving between both the commercial and artistic worlds, he was choreographer and stage director for numerous music artists, including Earth, Wind and Fire, Ashford and Simpson, and Gladys Knight. In his role as artistic director of the Faison Firehouse Theater in Harlem, he continues to pass on the legacy of the arts and cultural expression to inspired young dancers and performers within the industry, both in America and internationally.

Original poster for George Faison Universal Dance Experience. GEORGE FAISON

Musical theatre has also presented a doorway for many more female choreographers to make a name as commercial theatre dance creatives within a highly male-dominated arena. Here are some more names that are considered game-changers and innovators for modern musical theatre over the last thirty years.

George Faison Universal Dance Experience 1973 performing *Jesus Children* from *Only The Righteous Dancers*. Left to right: Paul Hoskins, Gary DeLotach, George Faison, LeVon Campbell, James Thurston. GEORGE FAISON

Twyla Tharp (1941–)

Tharp was a student and trained under Merce Cunningham and Martha Graham, later joining the innovative Paul Taylor Dance Company. In 1965, she formed her own dance company, Twyla Tharp Dance.

Tharp's first work on Broadway was *When We Were Very Young* (1980), followed by a collaboration with musician David Byrne on *The Catherine Wheel* and later *Singin' In The Rain*. In 2002, she created the dance musical *Movin' Out*, set to the music and lyrics of Billy Joel and later worked with Bob Dylan's music and lyrics on *The Times They Are A-Changin'* and *Come Fly Away*, set to songs sung by Frank Sinatra.

In film, her choreographic works include *Hair*, *Ragtime*, *Amadeus* and the 1985 dance film *White Nights* starring Gregory Hines and Mikhail Baryshnikov. For TV, her choreography has featured in the inaugural episode of *Dance in America* (1976). Tharp also co-produced and directed *Making Television Dance*, *The Catherine Wheel* (BBC), and co-directed the television special *Baryshnikov by Tharp*.

Tharp has created dance works for many established dance companies, which include The Joffrey Ballet, American Ballet Theatre, The Paris Opera Ballet, The Royal Ballet, New York City Ballet, The Australian Ballet, Hubbard Street Dance Chicago and The Martha Graham Dance Company.

Susan Stroman (1954–)

Stroman has achieved immeasurable commercial success through much of her career, earning nine Tony Awards, Drama Desk Awards and Olivier Awards for her work as both a director and choreographer on Broadway and London's West End.

Having trained as a dancer in ballet, jazz and tap dance, she had a successful career as a performer in theatre and dance musicals. She began her career as a theatrical choreographer on the off-Broadway show *Flora the Red Menace*. From here Stroman went on to achieve commercial and international success as a choreographer and director on Broadway with *Show Boat*, which reintroduced the Charleston dance to a new generation of theatre audiences. Other hit musical theatre shows include *Crazy for You* and *The Producers* and, more recently, *The Scottsboro Boys* and *Young Frankenstein*.

In keeping with most modern jazz dance choreographers, the fusion and influences of differing dance styles has enabled Stroman to crossover into the classical world with her a full-length ballet *Double Feature* for the New York City Ballet.

Dame Gillian Lynne DBE (1926–2018)

Lynne began her dance career as a ballet dancer, rising to prominence with the London company of Sadler's Wells Ballet. Her career has spanned over sixty years as a dancer, choreographer, director and producer. She is most remembered for her collaboration as choreographer with Andrew Lloyd Webber on his hit musical *Cats*. Lynne's previous experience as a choreographer brought together a fusion of classical, contemporary and elements of jazz dance. She followed *Cats* with *Phantom of the Opera* and *Aspects of Love*. Lynne also choreographed and staged the original musical theatre production of *Chitty Chitty Bang Bang* in London's West End. Gillian Lynne was one of the few female British musical theatre choreographers to make a real impact on British dance theatre.

Kimberlee Collicutt and Andrew Denton performing a narrative dance scene set to jazz blues music from the BOP Jazz Theatre production *Blues in the Night.*

Arlene Phillips CBE (1943–)

From her formative dance training, Phillips took her inspiration from American modern jazz dance of the 1970s. Through presenting her own jazz dance classes at Pineapple dance studio, and at performing colleges such as Italia Conti, the Phillips' jazz dance style and name came to prominence with training and professional dancers and the theatre world.

Her big break came as choreographer and director of her dance group Hot Gossip, which she formed in 1974 with dance students she was teaching. Hot Gossip became the featured dance group on the *Kenny Everett TV Show* and that led to their own TV show *The Very Hot Gossip* produced by Channel Four Television. Phillips' concepts and stylistic form of Hot Gossip took jazz dance on to a new platform and further raised her success as a female choreographer on UK television. Phillips' foray into musical theatre as choreographer was on the original film musical *Annie* (1982). This lead to original choreography on numerous UK and international musical productions, namely *Starlight Express*, *Saturday Night Fever*, *Grease* and *Flash Dance*. Her breadth of work has taken her from the stage to film, documentaries, light entertainment, a judge on *Strictly Come Dancing*, charity work and prestigious award nominations.

With a new generation of theatre creatives, the musical theatre shows that are now inspiring and influencing the jazz dance aesthetic in a more overt manner are predominantly black musical theatre productions. *Dreamgirls*, *Memphis*, *Motown* and *The Lion King* are all musical theatre productions that present African-American creative sensibilities and jazz dance expression to a wider audience demographic.

BOP company performing their original contemporary jazz theatre work *Daughters of Eve*.

BAFANA SOLOMAN MATEA

Adding to the black creative aesthetic in the current climate of musical theatre is the ground-breaking hip-hop dance narrative of the musical theatre production *Hamilton*. The choreographer of the musical, Andy Blankenbuehler, has become a name that a new generation of dancers and performers can now identify with. Blankenbuehler is now recognized and hailed for his innovative choreographic work and concepts for his celebrated Broadway and West End musical productions of *Hamilton*. His other creative works include *In the Height*, *Bandstand*, *Annie*, *9 to 5* and the revival of *Cats*. He has achieved numerous nominations and titles from Tony Awards to Olivier Awards. His refreshing and innovative choreographic vision is very much influenced and inspired by the rich lineage of jazz dance and modern jazz styles, fused with the form of hip-hop theatre and wrapped around musical theatre production sensibilities.

THE CONCEPTION OF CONCERT DANCE

For clarity in differing parts of the world, particularly the UK and Europe, concert dance is now aligned with performance theatre or show dance.

In parallel with musical theatre dance, there was concert theatre dance. The concept provided another avenue for the development of jazz dance and the work of creative modern dance theatre visionaries. Concert dance opened a channel to explore, develop and produce original, inspired, narrative dance works for the theatre.

As both musical theatre and concert dance developed as artistic forms, there became a distinction between both the creative approach and expression. Concert dance creatives looked to develop a style and technique that reflected their individual creative expression, not restricted by the set narratives of commercial music theatre productions. Consequently, many pioneers of concert dance established their own artistic dance companies, where, over time, they were able to develop and consolidate their individual styles and informed dance techniques.

IN THEIR OWN WORDS...

An aesthetic vision has to be present, a desirable goal that is not based upon gaining notoriety, money, or acceptability but is based upon reaching the aesthetic vision.... That doesn't mean starving, but it does mean that a group or a dancer has to have a standard, a level, a goal that is beyond the demands of the general culture.

Martha Graham

Artistic dance companies began to come into frame through the 1930s onwards, a number establishing creative approaches, dance styles and techniques that are still used by choreographers and dance creatives today.

In the early modern dance era, there were many differing practitioners creating artistic concert dance that delivered two differing artistic approaches, cultural expressions, creative styles and dance techniques. On one hand, there was American concert dance that spoke from the white perspective of classical/contemporary dance narrative, such as Isadora Duncan, George Balanchine and Martha Graham. On the other hand, there was African-American concert dance that spoke from the black narrative, such as Katherine Dunham, Alvin Ailey and Donald McKayle.

The companies expressing the African-American traditions were greatly influenced by the jazz tradition. Many incorporated this wholly into their individual dance narratives, others adapted elements of the jazz dance aesthetic to develop new modern dance styles and techniques.

There is a rich source of jazz dance influences by past jazz choreographers and dancers. This has provided a rich pool of alternative creative and artistic concepts to explore within the jazz dance art form. Unlike any other dance form, jazz offers an inclusive tapestry and represents a real diversity and delivery of the individual and collective creative expression.

Dollie Henry and Paul Jenkins performing an improvised jazz music and jazz dance work *Fusion*. SCOTT JORDANE

The Jazz Pioneers of Concert Dance

There are many choreographers and creative directors, both past and present, who deserve acknowledgment. Some names are easily recognized and others less so. However, each in their own right has left their artistry, vision, techniques and educational outreach of the jazz art form. Their works continue to offer inspiration to generations of dancers and choreographers who follow their creative and artistic legacy and contribution to the development of concert jazz dance.

Katherine Dunham (1909–2006)

Dunham is one of the few black female creative dance pioneers, innovators and academics of her generation, honoured with the title of the Grand Mistress of Jazz Dance Technique.

Dunham was a fully trained dancer in classical ballet, modern dance, and African, Caribbean, East Asian and Polynesian dance forms. In 1931, aged just twenty-one years old, she formed her own company, Ballets Nègres, one of the first black dance theatre companies to be formed and recognized in the USA. Following the opening of her first dance school Dunham reformed her dance company, renaming it The Negro Dance Company (1933). While developing her company, Dunham was able to cross over to film and theatre, choreographing the film musical *Stormy Weather* (1943) in which she featured along with her dancers.

As an anthropologist, dance ethnologist and

IN THEIR OWN WORDS…

I had certain physical limitations that made me change the choreography for myself or made me more interested in choreography only rather than dancing. I have never been a person who wanted to just dance. I have always been interested in developing for other people.

Katherine Dunham

academic, she studied and researched the differing dance styles from the Caribbean islands of Haiti, Jamaica, Trinidad and Martinique, as well as the dances of Europe, East Asia and South America. She used her research to inform, blend and incorporate into her individual choreographic expression. Dunham's dance style and choreographic innovation are acknowledged as important forces and factors in the forward movement of the modern jazz theatre dance aesthetic.

In 1945, the Katherine Dunham School of Dance and Theatre opened in New York, which went to be accredited as the Katherine Dunham School of Cultural Arts. The school itself was to become one of the most innovative establishments of its kind for creative dance and theatre of the time, out of which the Dunham dance technique was devised and developed, and is still taught today as a modern theatre dance technique and aesthetic. Katherine Dunham, with her influence and legacy, remains as a black female role model and icon for her multi-diverse approach and fusion of classical, modern, African, ethnic and jazz dance techniques and teachings.

Pearl Primus (1919–94)

Primus was yet another important figure in the elevation and awareness of African-American theatre dance. A dancer, choreographer, director, anthropologist and educator, she was instrumental in the evolution and development of theatre dance that represented the life and culture of black America, Africa and the Caribbean.

Originally from the Caribbean Island of Trinidad, at the age of two she arrived in New York with her parents. She was formally trained in classical and neo-classical ballet, and studied contemporary dance under Martha Graham and Doris Humphreys. She was a dancer with the New York-based dance company New Dance Group and performed on Broadway and in many concert performances, which she also choreographed. She formed her own company through which she was able to bring her work to a wider audience, with tours and high-profile performances world-wide.

IN THEIR OWN WORDS...

Why do I dance? Dance is my medicine. It's the scream which eases for a while the terrible frustration common to all human beings who because of race, creed, or color, are 'invisible'. Dance is the fist with which I fight the sickening ignorance of prejudice.

Pearl Primus

Her dances and works shared narratives that took inspiration from her own cultural heritage found in African-American literature, poems and music rooted in African syncopation and polyrhythms, spirituals, blues and jazz music. Her creative works have been performed by the Alvin Ailey American Dance Theater – *The Wedding* (1961) and *Fanga* (1949) – and she continues to hold the mantle for expanding the education of African dance studies in America, receiving numerous titles, honours and accolades for her contribution to African-American theatre dance and dance education, both in America and globally.

Alvin Ailey (1931–89)

Ailey is a name that all dancers know, whether jazz and ballet, black or white. Internationally renowned and respected, Ailey is a formidable giant of artistic concert dance theatre and a founder of one of the world's most celebrated creative dance institutions, the Alvin Ailey American Dance Theater (AAADT).

Ailey's vision for artistic and concert theatre dance has become a recognized aesthetic, style and expression that has coherently fused the dance vocabulary of his African-American heritage and creative expression, and the dance aesthetic of classical and modern contemporary dance.

His great influence came during his time training and performing with modern dance teacher/choreographer Lester Horton. He also trained under Martha Graham and Katherine Dunham. Ailey honed his career dancing in Broadway shows and was

IN THEIR OWN WORDS...

To be who you are and become what you are capable of is the only goal worth living.

Alvin Ailey

a lead dancer in the Broadway musical *Jamaica*, choreographed by Jack Cole and starring Hollywood film actress and singer Lena Horne.

In 1958, with a small group of dancers, Ailey went on to create and brand his self-named dance theatre company (AAAT). His mission for the company was to express black cultural heritage and find a platform in American dance that elevated black dance to the status of classical dance. Although the company explored and shared the black experience, Ailey employed dancers of all ethnicities. It is noted that he wanted the best dancers for his company and booked dancers based on their ability, rather than the colour of their skin.

His choreography offers a mix of dance styles and techniques taken from African-American dance, jazz dance, ethnic dances, ballet and modern (contemporary). His most famous and popular work *Revelations*, represents the music and movement of black spirituals, gospel, jazz and work songs, and is captured through dance that shows the commentary of African-American life. His company works and dancers from past to present are still hailed as some of the best dancers and performers in the world of modern theatre dance.

Donald McKayle (1930–2018)

Born in New York, McKayle's life experience, both from the diversity and racism present in America, had a great impact on his childhood. This greatly influenced much of his dance impression as a dance creative and director. Following on from the traditions of the Harlem Renaissance, McKayle was able to put to the front of his creativity the black American experience through his narrative and theatrical dance repertoire.

In his formative years as dancer, McKayle performed on Broadway, notably in the original Broadway production (1957) of *West Side Story* and was a celebrated dancer with modern choreogra-

Adam Parson Commonality Dance Company (USA) creating a strong masculine image enhanced by effective lighting. Dancers Shannon Holtzapffel, Lachlan McCarthy, Andrew Diolata, David Contreras, Michael Stein.
COMMONALITY DANCE COMPANY

IN THEIR OWN WORDS...

I always begin a project with the knowledge that I am dealing with people.

Donald McKayle

phers, Martha Graham, Merce Cunningham and Anna Sokolow.

During his career in 1951, he founded his dance company, Donald McKayle and Dancers. The company, with his vision for black dance, is recognized as one of the early exponents of concert theatre dance. His work and style encompassed the many extensions of African-American dance styles, modern jazz, contemporary (modern) and classical dance. His acclaimed concert dance works include *Games* (1951), *Round My Shoulder* (1959) and *District Storyville* (1962).

On Broadway, he achieved a number of Tony Award nominations as choreographer and/or director on the musicals *Golden Boy* starring Sammy Davis Jr and the musical production of *Raisin*. Other productions followed with *Doctor Jazz*, a musical theatre production featuring the music of jazz trumpeter 'King' Joe Oliver and the acclaimed *Sophisticated Lady*, a musical review that featured the music of jazz composer Duke Ellington.

His vast experience and work extended beyond dance theatre into film and TV. His choreography for films include *Bedknobs and Broomsticks*, *Jazz Singer* and *The Great White Hope*; and on TV, *The Johnny Carson Show*. His creative works have been performed by many international dance companies from the Alvin Ailey Dance Theater to the Limon Dance Company. McKayle has left an impressive legacy and is respected as one of the bright lights of modern concert dance theatre.

Dianne McIntyre (1946–)

McIntyre has led a respected and vast career over four decades and continues to work internationally as a choreographer, performer and director. Her creative work and expression of dance movement and dance theatre takes inspiration from, and is informed by, the consciousness of the black experience, often reflecting the great tradition emulating from the Harlem Renaissance of New York. Her creative journey brought collaborations with major jazz musicians and composers Olu Dara, Max Roach and Ahmed Abdullah, with the aim to find and express a more fluid connection between dance and jazz music.

Her influences extended to both avant-garde and free-style jazz. In 1972, Ms McIntyre founded her own dance theatre company, Sounds in Motion, based in Harlem, through which she continued to create her own concert dance works and put into motion the Sounds in Motion Dance School. As a performing company, with her dancers and musicians, she achieved great success both nationally and internationally. For over twenty years her creative dance studio in Harlem was to become an inclusive, creative hub for aspiring and established creative dance and music practitioners, poets and writers.

Her creative dance works have been performed by many recognized and established national and international dance theatre companies, including the Alvin Ailey Dance Theater, Dance Theatre of Harlem and Philidanco. On Broadway, her credits include *Mule Bone* and in the West End *King the*

IN THEIR OWN WORDS...

Sounds in Motion in Harlem in the seventies and eighties was a space not just for dancers and musicians, but became a center for what McIntyre calls, 'the culture crowd,' where many artists, scholars, activists would gather to forward the movement of Black consciousness. Here, McIntyre became a mentor to many promising artists, some of whom are now prominent dancers, choreographers, educators and founders of their own companies.

Dianne McIntyre

Terri Best Dance Company performing the jazz concert dance *Tick of the Clock*. The image shows the vitality of an extended jazz kick with all dancers performing in unison. From the 6th Annual Pasadena Dance Festival, Pasadena Civic Auditorium, April 2013. DENISE LEITNER

Musical and the English National Opera's (ENO) 2018 production of *Porgy and Bess*.

Ms McIntyre has been honoured with numerous accolades and awards throughout her prestigious career for her innovative work and presence in black dance and continues to work extensively as a major female creative force of concert theatre dance.

Gus Giordano (1923–2008)

Born in Chicago, Giordano's name is prominently associated with jazz dance education and the preservation of the jazz dance aesthetic and expression. His formative years' training began with ballet and modern (contemporary) dance. He further trained under Katherine Dunham and a number of established dance educators and choreographers. His professional career as a performer took him to New York, performing in off-Broadway and Broadway productions, including *On the Town*, *Guys and Dolls* and *The Pajama Game*. His work as a choreographer and producer led to bringing jazz dance to the small TV screen with programming of his dance series entitled *Jazz Dance*, which aired on the TV channel WTTW based in Chicago. His commercial production work enabled him to establish a highly inclusive platform for modern jazz dance.

It is through his dedication and impulse to present jazz as a valid dance form that he is best recognized. In 1953, he founded the Gus Giordano Dance School. The school was one of the very first jazz dance education establishments in America. Through his educational outreach and the development of his jazz dance technique and presence, he was able to influence and inspire a whole generation of jazz teachers, choreographers, professional dancers and dance students, actors and musicians. His legacy continues not only through his school, but his dance company. In 1963, he formed the Gus

Giordano Jazz Dance Chicago, which was later renamed the Gus Giordano Dance Chicago, now under the artistic directorship of his daughter, Nan Giordano.

Giordano was very much rooted in the authentic jazz dance aesthetic and was one of the first jazz dance creators to articulate his philosophy and teachings in the written form. His first jazz dance technique book was *Anthology of American Jazz Dance*, presented through pictures and an explanation that sought to articulate jazz dance. He followed this with *Jazz Dance Class: Beginning Thru Advanced*. This book explained jazz warm-ups, techniques and differing styles.

Leading on from his great educational works, in 1990 Giordano founded the first American Jazz Dance World Congress. The dance event is a celebration of the American art form of jazz dance. The event is over five days and brought together national and international jazz practitioners, dancers and students to share and participate in all things jazz dance.

IN THEIR OWN WORDS...

Jazz dance is a living art form, changing with the fashion of the times, but its roots remain in the original classic jazz method, which never goes out of style.

Gus Giordano

Giordano's method greatly influenced and laid the pathway for the jazz dance exercises, technique and theories of jazz dance educationalists Luigi Falco and Matt Mattox.

Performance of the narrative jazz theatre repertoire *Footprints in Jazz*, capturing the feeling of a community in reverence and reflection accentuated by powerful lighting.

CHAPTER 5

THE TAPESTRY OF JAZZ DANCE IN THE TWENTY-FIRST CENTURY

THE CHANGING LANDSCAPE OF JAZZ DANCE

At times, it is almost impossible to quantify what can be identified as jazz dance in our present dance landscape. This has created a hybrid of interpretations that are now often considered buds of the jazz dance tree. If you ask any creative, teacher or dancer to explain jazz dance, it takes some serious thinking and deliberation. Often no two answers would be the same. This is not surprising as jazz has, in many ways, become a victim of its own success.

As an inclusive art form, there are no barriers to being accepted into the jazz art family. Indeed, the new and the innovative has always kept the art form alive and moving forward, essential elements in the progressive development of jazz. However, it is increasingly apparent that students, audiences and even practitioners get confused when identifying the aesthetics of jazz dance today. Jazz dance has almost become an art form that accommodates all other dance expressions that are not considered ballet or contemporary.

As I travel the world delivering workshops and masterclasses, I am amazed as to how many dance classes I witness that are marketed as jazz dance but express none of the core techniques and aesthetics that are prevalent in jazz dance. This has caused confusion. Indeed, part of the aim of this book is to clearly identify jazz dance, establishing the root of the jazz aesthetic and then identify the differing branches of the jazz dance tree we witness today. It is essential that the inclusive nature of jazz does not shift the core voice of the art form, transforming the aesthetic to be almost unrecognizable as a form of jazz dance.

As jazz dancers, educators and creative practitioners, it is essential that we can identify the core expression and aesthetic of jazz dance. If you have read through the book, then you now have an understanding of the history of the jazz dance legacy and the creative approach needed to artistically express and deliver the art form.

As jazz has needed to survive through its commercial exploitation, it is not surprising that many of the developing jazz dance derivatives have a commercial emphasis. This does not mean jazz is not great art. The 'high art police' have long been confined to their barracks.

DEFINING THE JAZZ STYLES AND DERIVATIVES

For the serious jazz dance practitioner and student dancer, it is imperative to acquire and develop an overview of present-day jazz dance derivatives and the ability to identify them. This is especially important for educators, so that there is clarity when identifying particular jazz dance styles and aesthetics. Even though we pride ourselves on inclusivity as

OPPOSITE: **Spanish dancer Maia Rose Roberts in a stylized jazz pose.** NIKKI ROBERTS

jazz dance creators, there has to be an understanding and a creative level to our dance outcomes. Inclusivity does not mean 'open to any dance aesthetic', otherwise jazz dance will simply become a poor form of interpretive physical dance.

To simplify and help recognize the differing derivatives and styles of present-day jazz dance, this list provides a reference point. The list is not exhaustive, but will hopefully assist in identifying the main branches representative of the jazz dance idiom in the twenty-first century.

- Artistic jazz theatre
- Lyrical jazz
- Musical theatre
- Commercial and show dance
- Street and urban jazz dance
- Hip-hop dance theatre
- Afro-beat and dancehall
- Afro-Cuban and Latin jazz fusion

Artistic Jazz Theatre

Artistic jazz theatre is a natural extension and the present-day development of concert dance. The artistic philosophy behind jazz theatre provides the jazz practitioner with an opportunity to develop an artistic and creative approach to their jazz work, with the aim of creating original dance theatre that represents and reflects the artistic merit of the jazz dance idiom.

Of all the modern jazz dance derivatives, artistic jazz theatre is sometimes the least recognizable. This is in part due to confusion over its name. Artistic jazz theatre is particularly evident in the USA and Canada, where it is more readily identified and, therefore, artistically supported. In the UK and areas of Europe, the presence of artistic jazz dance theatre companies is still developing.

Internationally, there are present-day jazz practitioners who, individually and collectively, through their own body of work and teachings follow and share this philosophy. As jazz practitioners, there is a commitment in following the artistic response and interpretation of the jazz dance idiom, to produce and create original jazz theatre works that reflect the legacy and future of the jazz idiom, further developing the artist arc of the jazz cannon.

Jazz Dance Theatre Companies

- Adam Parson – Commonality Jazz Dance Company (LA/USA)
- Bob Boross – Bob Boross Freestyle Jazz (NYC/USA)
- Camille A. Brown – Camille A. Brown and Dancers (NYC/USA)
- Dollie Henry and Paul Jenkins – BOP Jazz Theatre Company (London/UK)
- Geraldine Armstrong – Armstrong Jazz Ballet (Paris/France)
- Joan Mayers Brown – The Philadelphia Dance Company (Philadnco) (Philadelphia/USA)

BOP Jazz company, music and dance.

SIMON RICHARDSON

Dollie Henry performing *Footprints in Jazz.*
BRENDON HANSFORD

- Kimberley Cooper – Decidedly Jazz Dance Works (Calgary/Canada)
- Melanie George – Jazz Is... Dance Project (USA)
- Nan Giordano – Giordano Dance (Chicago/USA)
- Pat Taylor – Jazz Antiqua Dance and Music Ensemble (LA/USA)
- Natasha Powell – Holla Jazz (Toronto/Canada)
- Raza Hammadi – Ballet Jazz Art (Paris/France)
- Reginald Ray-Savage – Savage Jazz (California/USA)
- Rick Odums – Ballet Jazz Company (Paris/France)
- Stephanie Heroux – Jazz Inc. Dance (Boston/USA)
- Sue Samuels – Jazz Roots Dance Company (NYC/USA)
- Terri Best – Terri Best Dance Co. (LA/USA)

Lyrical Jazz Dance

Originally, lyrical jazz was a term that came from the development of modern dance. As jazz dance became more commercial through the modern jazz era of the 1940s, the term lyrical jazz described and kept intact the artistic nature of jazz dance.

Lyrical jazz is more often viewed as narrative dance, where the movement of the body reflects a storyline or theme, enabling the dancer, through the choreography, to express the emotional content of the musical narrative. Jazz dance techniques are still the primary source of creativity in the choreography.

With the popularity and commercial exploitation of TV dance competitions, such as *So You Think You Can Dance*, the need to classify dance styles into an easily identifiable form was paramount. Therefore, in the public consciousness, lyrical jazz has simply become lyrical dance and is now an amalgam of jazz, contemporary, ballet and even acrobatics. That is not to say lyrical jazz in its original form no longer exists, it does. It certainly is not a dance interpretation to the lyrics of a song.

Carrie Willis performing a lyrical jazz dance *Flamenco Sketches* from the BOP Jazz Theatre production *Touches of Miles*. The image displays the influence of ballet in jazz dance with the extended line and position of a classical ponche. WILLIAM POTTER

Musical Theatre

Musical theatre in the twenty-first century is a phenomenon. However, its style and development has gone from musicals, where jazz was the main impetus of the dance experience, to dance that bears little or even no relevance to the jazz dance aesthetic.

Over the last twenty-five years or so, there has been an enormous explosion of musical theatre productions. These musicals have a diverse variety of styles and settings reflecting the many changes of music and dance styles that have developed over the decades.

Both on Broadway (USA) and the West End stages (UK), many musicals have enjoyed amazing commercial success. There are the large-scale productions, such as *Les Miserables*, *Miss Saigon*, *Phantom of the Opera*, *Evita* and *Cats*, which display dance that is more of a fusion of styles. They make use of more classical, contemporary and show-dance techniques as the main dance aesthetic, with the occasional influence of a jazz dance expression. For the choreographer, these types of musicals are often narrative and offer a rich creative palette for dance expression. The dance shares equal footing with the singing and acting.

Interestingly there is still great commercial appetite for musical theatre rooted in the jazz dance aesthetic. Many theatre producers remount successful musical theatre shows that allow new audiences an opportunity to see classic musical theatre. The dance styles of these musical theatre productions have a direct linage to the jazz dance idiom; for example, *Chicago*, *Sweet Charity*, *West Side Story*, *Chorus Line*, *Guys and Dolls*, *Top Hat* and *Dreamgirls*.

Fosse dancer, Alex Frei, in a still pose from the Fosse musical *Dancing*. TATJANA JENTSCH

More recently, we have witnessed the rise of the pop musical format. These theatre shows reinterpret successful pop music back catalogues and chart hits as the main emphasis of the production. Musicals such as *Mama Mia*, *Grease*, *We Will Rock You*, *Saturday Night Fever*, *Bat out of Hell* and *Footloose* all flow from this devised format. The dance narrative is generally more aligned with commercial dance derivatives or show dance, again making the jazz dance expression and aesthetic less noticeable.

There are also the musicals that are rooted and driven by black narrative and expression, such as *Five Guys Named Moe*, *Memphis*, *Motown*, *Dreamgirls*, *Tina* and *The Lion King*. These musicals deliver a dance aesthetic more akin to the black tradition and cultural expression of the jazz dance idiom. More importantly, these musicals provide a visual narrative of dance that reflects the essence of the music.

Bringing us up to date, the biggest change in the way dance for musicals has developed is with the Broadway and West End production of the multi-award winning *Hamilton*. This is a ground-breaking musical theatre production, which has created and established a new energy with a fusion of hip-hop dance styles. The lineage of hip-hop dance theatre is very much rooted in jazz expression and it is exciting to witness the most recent extension of the black dance derivatives. Equally important, for the development of musical theatre, *Hamilton* is also an original production and not a revival. It has single-handedly provided a mainstream platform in musical theatre for hip-hop theatre, reaching a much wider musical theatre and dance audience demographic.

Choreographers also leaving their mark on musical theatre over the last twenty years, who are to be acknowledged for their creative works and musical theatre recreations, include:

- Anthony Van Laast (UK)
- Bill Deamer (UK)
- Camille A. Brown (USA)
- Drew McOnie (UK)
- Kenny Ortega (USA)
- Karen Bruce (UK)
- Matthew Bourne (UK)
- Peter Darling (UK)
- Stephen Mear (UK)

Commercial and Show Jazz Dance

The style of commercial dance has always been closely related to jazz. From time as far back as minstrel shows, the commercial aspects of jazz entertainment have been fundamental to its survival, enabling it flourish on a populist cultural and social level.

The commercial dance industry is a fast-moving one, attempting to adapt to the latest trends and styles, music and even fashion. As times have changed, both style and creative approach has adapted. Today the style of commercial dance is no longer always aligned to the jazz dance aesthetic, but will be classified as having a jazz dance slant, mainly due to the nature of the work and its situation. This is evident in a great deal of music videos, where the image and look is the primary focus and the dance supports the visual image and content.

Commercial jazz dance certainly has its place in the pantheon of jazz dance styles and it is possibly where many more dancers are able to secure a steady and varied performing career. Commercial dance is apparent on many differing entertainment platforms, including: television and film, music industry and music videos, corporate shows, advertisement and product placement, fashion shows, cruise ships, competition show dance, so the list goes on. Versatility and a specific commercial look are essential for any dancer wishing to stake out a career in the commercial sector of the dance industry.

There are many choreographers pushing forward as commercial dance advocates – too many to list them all, but the following names should be mentioned:

- Brian Friedman (USA)
- Fatima Robinson (USA)
- Mia Michaels (USA)
- Michael Rooney (USA)
- Rich and Tone Talauega (USA)
- Laurieanne Gibson (USA)

The dancing feet of jazz. SIMON RICHARDSON

The Impact of Hip-hop/Urban Dance

As is now well documented, the dance styles of much of the urban dance genre primarily originated on the streets of America, from breakdancing to locking, from b-boying and krumping, to hip-hop theatre. This specific genre and style of dance is now established as an important creative dance expression.

As a dance form, hip-hop as an extension of jazz is very inclusive and its recent commercial exploitation has made the form increasingly popular and influential. However, unlike commercial dance, there is not so much emphasis on one particular 'look'. This has very much contributed to its rise in popularity. It often provides a creative community environment for youth culture and also the recreational dancer, as is evident in the many youth hip-hop troupes and urban dance collectives.

Although jazz and hip-hop are intrinsically linked, the training, many of the techniques, movement, styles, musical interpretation and choreography differ greatly. In keeping with its jazz lineage, hip-hop has always been an organic social expression, created through music, dance and song (poetry, the spoken word, rap). Indeed, rapping can be viewed as a continuation of the oral traditions of the African griots, passing down through history and culture as they travel from village to village. So without music there is no dance. It is important to recognize that hip-hop music and hip-hop dance developed in collaboration. Indeed, many of the early pioneers of hip-hop worked closely with music artists and early hip-hop producers. These pioneers include Don Campbell, Emillio 'Budda Stretch' Austin, Samuel Soloman, Ceasare Willis and Jo Ratti.

The very nature of both hip-hop and urban dance is that it changes rapidly as a new young generation of dance practition-

Joe Hunt performing *Cool* with stylized choreography fusing jazz and hip-hop dance.
BRENDON HANSFORD

ers seek to express their creative work through this genre. As with all modern trends in commercial music and dance, much of the groundwork still continues to be instigated, created and formed from the streets, in dance halls, clubs and halls, dance studios and rehearsal spaces. Each dance creator develops movements and a stylistic approach that represent their individuality and also the accompanying music. Eventually, the most popular style makes its way into the mainstream, inspiring another generation. For sure, nothing is new. Dance has been, and will always be, reinvented or assimilated into the current dance trends.

The effect of recent TV programmes, films and music videos has also afforded many urban/hip-hop creators and dancers a springboard to develop their work in the commercial arena.

There are a number of hip-hop dance groups that have emerged from TV exposure and these include the ever popular commercial UK hip-hop dance groups Flawless and Diversity.

Recently, there has been a rise in development of hip-hop theatre (not to be confused with *Hamilton*, which is a musical theatre production using hip-hop dance). This development places the dance in a more theatrical setting.

Hip-hop theatre can be traced back to the early 1990s when it was created and produced through the creative works of Rennie Harris (*So What Happens Now*, *Rome* and *Jewels*). In the UK, hip-hop performer, artistic director and choreographer Kenrick Sandy (artistic director of Boy Blue Entertainment), was leading the way as the first hip-hop theatre company to be recognized for the hip-hop theatre production *Pied Piper*.

Jonzi D, the curator of *Breakin' Convention*, and Hakeem Onibudo, associate producer at The Place, and female hip-hop practitioner Katie Prince and her company Zoonation, have gone on to achieve the support and opportunities to continue championing hip-hop theatre both in the UK and internationally.

Today hip-hop dance continues to ascend to new heights, influencing the majority of 'commercial dance' styles. Its reach has even stretched to contemporary dance and progressive ballet companies who use elements of urban/hip-hop dance in their new works created by hip-hop choreographer Rennie Harris. Other notable names include Shane Sparks, Wade Robson and Nacho Pop. Hip-hop has come a long way since its early inception from the urban streets of America to the most populist dance form of our time.

CHAPTER 6

JAZZ DANCE EDUCATION, TRAINING AND DEVELOPMENT

AN EDUCATIONAL OVERVIEW: BASIC TRAINING AND JAZZ DANCE VOCABULARY

Over the last thirty years, jazz dance has consistently proved to be one of the most popular and prominent dance styles taught in our dancing schools, dance colleges and part of dance study in our performing arts colleges and university dance courses.

In the UK, dancers are able to study jazz dance at all levels, from set syllabus examination boards (ISTD/IDTA) or through dance placed within sports and vocational study academic education (AQA/BTEC/A Level/GSCE Dance). There are also the many performing arts colleges providing HE, Foundation and BA degrees in jazz dance and universities offering MAs, DIPEd, HNCs, HNDs and PhDs.

The multiplicity of open studio jazz dance classes has become as diverse as the many dancer/teachers that proclaim jazz dance as their teaching identity. With the many differing approaches apparent, for the committed jazz dancer and student this can be particularly confusing.

The millennia generation of dancers do not always easily identify with a recognizable jazz dance technique and, consequently, are less sure of how to acquire one. I am increasingly asked for my opinion on training and development for the jazz dancer. The questions vary: What is the best jazz technique? What is the jazz dance aesthetic and where does it originate from? What is the perfect jazz dance warm-up? How to develop jazz choreography and where to find jazz music? Such questions are not surprising, given that jazz dance is now identified through a myriad of dance styles and forms today.

To help understand the correct approach, and as a point of reference, let's take a quick look at the requirements for classical dance. Here the aesthetic, technique and physical attributes for the dancer are very clear and concise. The training, vocabulary and technique have survived and developed over centuries. The teaching and the passing on of the art forms are presented by professional practitioners and specialists in that dance form. Ballet teachers and choreographers have a clear and detailed understanding of the legacy, and how to acquire and develop a technique that will enable the dancer to be successful in the ballet world. The same can be said of modern/contemporary dance, where specific dance styles and techniques are presented in their unique form, with the lineage and vocabulary intact, easily identifiable and recognizable.

IN THEIR OWN WORDS...

It takes an athlete to dance, but an artist to be a dancer.

Shanna LaFleur

OPPOSITE: **Dollie Henry.** SIMON RICHARDSON

If, as a dancer, creative inclination is toward jazz dance expression, it is important to have a real grasp of the true aesthetic and vocabulary of jazz dance. Appreciating and understanding the basic principles of jazz dance guides and supports the realization of a superior jazz dance technique, musical understanding and delivery of the resulting dance. The more versatile and inquisitive dancer will attend numerous dance classes, some focusing on the more commercial and urban styles, others the more artistic styles and yet others on musical theatre.

Jazz dance offers an easier route for the dancer to attain a working career, with many more opportunities for employment in the commercial show dance sector. Those wishing to seek out a career as an artistic dancer suited to the company (jazz) environment, sadly have fewer options to choose from. However, that does not mean jazz dance is not worthy of a real commitment. It is essential to consider what type of jazz dancer/artist you want to be. In this way, you can analyse the style and draw a conclusion as to the technique and skills needed and required for jazz dance. Jazz is fundamentally an expression of real life and so it has to become a creative lifestyle choice too.

Dollie leading dancers in a jazz warm-up.

Remember, the quality of training for the jazz dancer is dependent on the expertise, proficiency and erudition of the jazz teacher. Research and seek out the best teachers for you and your development as a dancer. It is through further creative investigation, analysis and intensive training that a deeper connection and understanding of the jazz aesthetic and expression of the dance form can be found. Taking time to explore jazz in all its creative wonder can only add to the dancer's individual development, enabling a foundation to create and perform jazz dance that is of real artistic and creative value.

DEVELOPING THE CORRECT SKILLS AND TECHNIQUES FOR JAZZ DANCE

Jazz dance will always be in a state of metamorphosis and so the same transition is inevitable for the jazz dancer. Whether a dance novice or a seasoned professional, the fact that the jazz dance art form is constantly evolving means that training methods and performance skills must inevitably change and grow too. Maintaining the body, both physically and mentally, is no different from that of a top athlete. Jazz dance is not unlike classical dance, in that it needs to be viewed and practised with real intent to develop to a proficient level technically, whilst developing intuitively and creatively. It is through the practical experience and visual understanding that provides the dancer with a point of reference to relate to, learn from and be inspired by.

Any dance study and training is a process of discovery and as with any creative endeavour, it takes time, energy and commitment. Remember, training the mind and the body is an ongoing practice for the serious dancer.

To stay in tip-top condition, continued training should be a compulsory rider note on every dancer's schedule. It is required more so when a dancer is in between work or working on a long contract. Many dancers find they lose their ability to retain choreography and the once solid technique, when not engaged in performing or through only dancing and performing one specific style for a long period of time.

IN THEIR OWN WORDS...

If you look at a dancer in silence, his or her body will be the music. If you turn the music on, that body will become an extension of what you're hearing.

Judith Jamison

Music, Musicality and Movement

For any dancer seeking to further refine their jazz artistry, it is important to grasp the essence of jazz music and get tuned-in. Jazz music for some can feel and sound quite intimidating. However, as you develop your aural skills and expand your listening capacity to capture the many derivatives of jazz music, you will find it inspiring and emotive, exciting and wonderful to dance to and create to.

I spend much of my time as a jazz teacher, reminding my students, and also my company dancers, to listen to the music. What defines a jazz dancer is their musical timing. Training the musical ear is as important as training the physical body. When a dancer is aurally connected to the music, the dance movement, steps and emotional connection within the choreography takes on a whole different meaning and feeling, both for the dancer and the onlooker.

A jazz dance class without jazz music defeats the process and purpose of jazz dance training. All my jazz classes and exercises are accompanied and supported by jazz music or its derivatives. The aim is to give dancers a means of listening to the music of jazz and to introduce their ears and physicality to the rhythms, beats, syncopation and pulse that drives and informs the dance and movements.

Jazz music and jazz dance have always had a symbiotic relationship. The marriage between the sound and the movement are inherently, spiritually and organically connected. Without a doubt, (jazz) music is an important and vital partner to the overall delivery and expression of jazz dance. There is no fundamental creative difference, aside from the fact that the musician uses their instrument to play and the dancer uses their body to share and express their art and, ultimately, themselves.

Tuning in to the music and really listening to the expression of each instrument and each musician performing, connecting to the musical conversation, is when you begin to hear the musical layers that provide a canvas upon which to paint the dance.

I am often asked at the end of my jazz classes and workshops, for the names of the jazz artists, jazz vocalists and title of a musical track I have used for the exercises or dance combinations. This proves that the energy of jazz music induces much more of a connection to the senses when we exercise and when we dance. Once there is an understand-

Sarah Dos Santos performing in BOP Jazz Theatre production *Miles Ahead*.

ing that, as jazz dancers, we are simply expressing the movement to the music, the dance can take on another meaning and we connect on a higher sensory level that is beyond the steps. As I remind all dancers, jazz dance is simply the physical and visual manifestation of jazz music.

Not so long ago, jazz music was the popular music of the times and provided the musical inspiration and direction for jazz dance classes of a certain creative calibre. As popular music has changed, so have the teachers and their teaching methods, which have also changed the direction and physicality of how the jazz dance aesthetic, movement and techniques are now perceived and practised to music.

Often the music heard pouring out of a dance studio for jazz classes is popular chart music, which in fairness bears little resemblance to the energy, rhythm and swing beat of jazz music. It is the music that dictates our ability to dance in time and it is the music that allows us to feel each motion of movement. Therefore, it is important that the jazz dancer experiences, from as early as possible, all types of music that fall under the jazz music banner.

Dancers from BOP jazz residency connecting to the music.

IN THEIR OWN WORDS...

Just live the music, it's the true inspiration for the creation of jazz dance.

Dollie Henry

The philosophy that drives the natural creative impulse of jazz musicians and jazz music (improvisation) works in exactly the same uncensored way for the creative impulse of the jazz choreographer or dancer. The thinking behind this is simple: if a group of musicians can play separately and yet come together as whole, this same process can be adopted by jazz dancers – the freedom to be an individual and yet be part of the whole experience. Jazz music is like food to the jazz dance, as it directs the dancer to find an emotional connectivity and symbiotic relationship between the music, the movement and the resulting dance and community play.

In many ways, jazz dance is like creating a painting. As jazz dancers, we can play it safe and just join the musical dots with a colouring pencil or we can get a great big paint brush, choose some amazing colours and shades, and create a jazz dance masterpiece.

I remind all my dancers and students that the study of jazz music can dictate how you perform and share yourself as a jazz dancer. Each time a piece of jazz music is listened to, there will be something in the music or musicianship that will be new to the ear and offer yet another musical vibration to create and dance upon. Connecting with the melodies, musical narrative and voicing of each instrument in jazz music will enable the dance to develop organically through the music. This way the dance stays fresh, innovative, spontaneous and alive. Jazz music is more than just a sound, it is the natural swing, pulse, timing and instinctive groove that underscores and expresses jazz dance aesthetic qualities.

There are so many differing styles and derivatives to be found in jazz music that offer an eclectic soundscape for delivering a true expression to jazz dance, be that in the exercise and training process, dance class combinations or creating jazz theatre dance for performance. Take time to enlighten the musical ear and let the sounds and instrumental conversations speak back to you or just simply let the music take you on a journey of discovery.

THE MAIN PRINCIPLES AND CODES OF THE JAZZ DANCE EXPRESSION

Although we recognize jazz dance as a fusion of dance styles, the outward expression is distinguished by specific principles and codes founded within the original root of the jazz dance expression.

Jazz dance is defined by its aesthetic and kinetic qualities. Although these core qualities are becoming less identifiable in jazz dance today, they still punctuate the main elements that are a prerequisite in identifying the jazz technique, its styles, physicality, vitality and musicality, keeping a link to the roots of the jazz expression.

The aesthetic qualities (visual) are:

- Improvisational
- Intuitive and individual
- Freedom of expression
- Musical (rhythm/timing)
- Call and response (communication)
- Participatory (community)
- Celebratory
- Dynamic
- Emotive
- Narrative (storytelling)

The kinetic qualities (movement) are:

- Centrifugal strength (core power)
- Grounded (earth bound)
- Flatter-footed

Dollie Henry in the rehearsal process showing her dancers the energy and dynamics required for the emotive expression of the choreography.
SLAVO VALASTEK

- Use of plié
- Flexible
- Athletic
- Agile
- Spontaneous
- Responsive and receptive
- Rhythmical fluidity

For a dancer at the beginning of their jazz dance journey, defining the basic movements, terms and vocabulary will assist in achieving a higher level of technique and enlightened understanding of the practice of jazz dance.

The terminology to describe many of the steps and movements used in jazz dance are aligned to the terminology used for classical dance. It is important to remember that jazz is now an amalgam of differ-

Dancers executing an athletic jazz kick, which shows the use of the grounded plié on the supporting leg, so providing extra strength and agility to execute the kick with spontaneous action.

ing dance expressions, techniques and styles that have been set into a standard dance language. This universal language assists teaching practices and identifies the specific dance steps and movement.

APPLYING THE JAZZ TECHNIQUE THROUGH STEPS AND MOVEMENT

For the jazz dance beginner, there are some very useful and much used steps in jazz dance that are worth becoming familiar with. Understanding the purpose and attaining the skills to particular jazz dance steps and movements enable the dancer to find the dexterity, coordination and dynamics of the dance. It is essential to learn the technique of weight transference, which enables a fluidity of dance movement when responding to the tempo, rhythms and dynamics of the accompanying music. How we use the body is based upon the dance skills and techniques that we practise regularly.

The Plié

The plié is a prerequisite of jazz dance and can be viewed as the 'oil in the legs' for the quality of movement when we dance. More important, the plié is a natural technique associated to the aesthetic and kinetic display of jazz dance.

We generally assume the understanding of the plié as a form of exercise that forms part of a more technical exercise for the physical warm-up. In jazz

The plié in jazz dance assists flexibility of movement allowing the dancer to become more adaptable and less restricted in movement.

The plié provides a flow of movement and freedom for the dancer when in action.

dance, the plié is also used as a transferable technical dance skill and characteristic of movement that defines the jazz dance aesthetic.

Often dancers assume that using the plié in dance means to crouch or squat down into the legs – quite the opposite. The use of the plié in jazz dance provides a deeper flexibility of the legs to move rhythmically and spontaneously without hesitation. The natural use of the plié, allows for a natural flow, a fluidity of movement and assistance when transferring from one step to another with ease and dexterity.

Fine-tuning of the plié movement through dance training develops the muscular power and strength of the legs and dynamic of movement.

As already mentioned, the plié and the use of it in jazz dance is one of the natural techniques that defines the flow, smoothness and buoyancy of movement, and allows for greater control to execute jazz steps that are executed at speed and can be executed with on-point timing and control of movement.

The plié in use and position as shown in this image of the dancers in a jazz hinge position.

The plié is often used in jazz choreography and can create a powerful image and position in dance choreography. SIMON RICHARDSON

A simple way to recognize what differentiates the aesthetics of jazz dance and ballet dance:

- The classical leg line is developed to straighten and pull up out of the legs and body, to accentuate elegant lines and give a sense of elevation and movement above the floor, airbound.
- Jazz is the opposite, executed through the plié, giving a look and placement of movement closer to the floor, rooted, earthbound.

Jazz Walks

It may sound obvious to the advanced dancer, but jazz walks for the beginner are a sure-fired way for a dancer to find their natural coordination of movement, to understand timing and musicality. The look and feel of a jazz walk is grounded into the floor and can be danced in varying ways from slow and lyrical to fast and dynamic.

Arm movements, shoulders and other dance steps and turns can be interwoven to assist and develop coordination, timing, musicality and individual dance expression. Another term used to describe a jazz walk is drag walk and for speed of movement, jazz runs.

Dancers executing jazz runs that create a gliding moving across the floor.

Jazz walks can be adapted in style and purpose within dance and choreography.

Jazz Pas de Bourée

This is one of the most adaptable and useful steps in the jazz dance canon, which can be used in a variety of differing ways. A three-step move, it allows for weight distribution and transference of weight from one foot to the other. It is an ideal transitionary step in jazz dance and can be performed straight forward, turning or to the side. The pas de bourée is also a very effective travelling step and is used as a preparation step for pirouettes and jumps, and is an easy step to adapt through musical interpretation and timing in choreography.

Step Ball Change

Everyone who has ever danced will know the sequence of steps that make up a standard step ball change. This is another staple of jazz dance and is very much like the pas de bourée. This is a

The chassé position in movement.

Box step – movement 1.

sequence of steps that again transfers the weight from one foot to the other. It requires a sense of coordination and understanding of balance transfer. It is a sequence of three steps that transfers the weight to the ball of the other foot and transfers the weight back to the first foot. Again, the speed of the step ball change can vary and change in interpretation, depending on how the step is used. It can be used as a travelling step, on the spot step, used as a turning step, transitional or preparation step into another dance movement.

The Chassé Movement

The word derives from the classical dance vocabulary. The movement is used in jazz dance in the same way as in ballet, to move across the floor. In practice, the jazz chassé uses the plié to push through into movement used to travel and find impetus to move across the floor. The chassé is a useful and much used transitional movement that connects dance steps and the movement will vary in dance, depending on how it is placed in context to the sequence of exercise or choreography and musical timing.

The 'Box' Step and Drag Step

This an old school jazz step that is still used in jazz

Drag step.

dance to great effect. It is an easy step for a beginner to learn. As the name describes, this sequence of four steps creates a floor pattern movement in the shape of a box.

The figure of foot movement:

1. Cross right foot over left foot
2. Step back on the left foot
3. Step to the side with the right foot
4. Step forward with the left foot

There are many movements and positions that cross over and are used in all the differing dance forms. However, as already mentioned, the movement, timing and execution will be defined by the actual aesthetic of the dance form. Jazz dance allows for manipulation of the movements when assimilating the aesthetic and kinetic strengths of jazz dance.

Extension of arms giving a sense of dynamics in movement relating to the beat of the music.

Finding and Feeling the Extension of the Movement

This is a term in jazz dance that is used to describe varying styles of movement that are generally aligned with the arms and leg movements and through the body. Finding an extension in a movement is defining a feeling that dictates a lengthening of the limbs in dance that extends outward and beyond the body. The movement of the extension gives a more pronounced defined line or emphasis to sustaining the movement of dance. It can also give an extra emotive quality and connection to the visual description and feel of the dance. To find the feeling of extension, imagine the energy of the movement going way beyond the fingers and toes when in movement, as if reaching far beyond the physical extremities.

Extension of movement shown through lyrical gesture, giving a sense of release in the upper body.

The movement of the release creates a sense of power and dynamics in the upper body position of the dancer.

Release and Let Go

The meaning behind the movement of a release is to let go within the body. It is a movement of dance that is used in jazz dance to add texture and feeling in choreography and exercise, and adds a moment of breath and freedom within sustained movements. It offers a feeling of light and shade to choreography and can be performed either as a dynamic movement or emotively, depending on the use in choreography and dance narrative.

The Hinge Positions

The hinge position is used in many variations for jazz dance. As a position of the body when in motion of dance, the hinge requires the dancer to have a strong core, thighs, legs and feet, as the whole body is used to create and control this position within the body.

The appearance of a hinge in movement is a feeling of being at an angle with the body line. It is not to be confused with a back bend, which is the curving

Dancers finding the upper body release from a floor position within the choreography.

Remy Martyn shows the hinge position using the whole body. SIMON RICHARDSON

The hinge position can give shape and a dynamic of lines within jazz dance.

of the spine. The feeling in the body and position of body line can vary, depending on flexibility and core control, but as a movement it offers a visually powerful and exciting position that can be used to give both a dynamic or lyrical expression in jazz dance choreography.

The Relevé Position

In jazz dance, the feet are the closest part of the body to the floor and are a way of connecting to a source energy used to give a grounded effect in jazz dance (earthbound). The relevé or rising up onto the ball of the foot, is used to dictate specific dance moves and positions, created to express the dance. It is essential that the dancer's feet, balls of foot, ankles and metatarsal muscles are developed to withstand quite vigorous use and positioning, to support specific jazz dance movements. Strengthening exercises and developing through practice of the jazz dance technique will help develop the feet, giving them their power and strength.

Low-lying flat hinge position.

Kneeling hinge position.

Jazz Pirouettes and Turning Step

Those that have studied dance from an early age will remember the basic turning on the spot exercises. The benefits of understanding the technique and use of the head and eyes to spot when delivering a pirouette, allows for greater preparation, accuracy and clarity to the start of the movement, right through to the end of the pirouette.

The core components to execute that perfect jazz pirouette are:

- Spotting
- Balance
- Core strength
- Plié
- Speed
- Confidence

Applying and Practising the Technique for a Jazz Pirouette

As the saying goes, you would not drive a car blind, so why dance blind! No matter what form and style of dance, the skill for perfecting a decent pirouette starts with a decent spotting technique. Spotting prevents dizziness and helps to guide the movement to its final direction and placement within the choreography.

From the Eurocentric development of the pirouette in dance, the interpretation is that of the straight leg position on the turning leg, as in classical dance. However, it is important to go back and look at the aesthetic of the jazz pirouette. With the knowledge and appreciation for the root of jazz dance, the placement and position of the jazz pirouette is grounded to the dance floor and connects with the energy from the ground up. The foot is naturally placed in a flatter position to the floor and not hypo-extended onto the full relevéd foot. A naturally placed foot promotes a closer connection for the placement of the pirouette and also provides a deeper control in the legs and the ability to adjust the speed of the pirouette in execution.

Samantha Tan shows how the relevé can be used when in dance movement. SIMON RICHARDSON

Pirouette position in plié.

As with all dance movements, it is through developing and understanding our body that advancement is made. The correct upper body placement, core discipline and control support a greater balance whilst in the motion of the pirouette. The skills and technique to execute a pirouette is used to the maximum. There are variations on a jazz pirouette but, as with all dance, a solid technique and understanding of the physical skills is required to attain and sustain.

For greater agility, speed and dynamics, the jazz pirouette is traditionally performed using a pliable (soft) plié on the working leg. It is the action and shape of a jazz pirouette that gives the effect of accurate timing and speed of revolution. This provides a jazz pirouette with the internal energy that is controlled, yet shows a confidence and freedom when in action. The aesthetic of the jazz pirouette produces a unique visual display that differentiates the movement to that used and performed in classical dance.

Mastering the jazz pirouette can bring an added flair and individuality for the dancer within performance. Harnessing the correct technique for a dancer at the beginning of their dance/jazz training is to first master and perfect a single pirouette as a foundation for development. For the advanced/professional jazz dancer, the sky is the limit for ongoing development for attaining the precision of technique to perform multiple revolutions, for double, triple and quadruple jazz pirouettes in various positions.

Dancers finding the preparation position for a jazz pirouette.

Alternative Pirouettes and Turning Steps

Pencil Turn

As the name quite easily identifies, the pencil turn requires the body to be pulled up to give the impression of looking like a pencil – elongated, slim and pivotal. The working leg on which the movement starts is positioned straight in the turn with the other leg aligned to the working leg to give the appearance of being centrally balanced in the pirouette and body. Depending on the use of this pirouette/turn in a creative situation, the arms can be lifted above the head, to give length to the body-line and movement, or as required to express dance.

The position of the whole body when executing a pencil turn.

Using a grounded preparation through the plié supports the action and energy of the kick in movement.

Knee Turn (Chainés Turn on the Knees)

This movement is performed like a basic chainé turn, but set and executed on one or both knees. A dancer will need sturdy knees to perform this specific dance move in jazz dance. It is important to keep the weight lifted in the body so as not to push the weight of the body into the knees and floor, causing discomfort or injury.

The Jazz Kick

For the jazz beginner it is important to learn the correct technique, so as not to injure and tear the muscles in the process, especially if not warmed up appropriately. Kicks need a certain power and strength from behind the leg (glutes and hamstring muscles) and also flexibility in the hips and good core strength, to allow for a kick to be executed with a dynamic impact and extension in flight of movement.

For the beginner, start with simple, low kicks, to find extension of the leg line and dynamic of movement, giving attention to working on finding the position of the body and preparation to execute the kick.

In kick exercises, by using the plié movement on preparation and breathing correctly, this allows for the movement of the leg to find the energy and ease, so as to sit in time with the style or energy of the music and dance. Kicks can be placed in front, to the side, to the back, in fact all around the body and there are many variations on a kick used in jazz.

As a sample, here are some of the more popular kicks that are achievable for the advanced and professional dancer. In isolation, kicks offer a dynamic strike and punch to the jazz cannon of dance movements.

Dancers executing a battement jazz kick exercise.

The Outward Round Kicks aka Fan Kick

The outward round kick is a variation of a kick used in jazz. The body is the anchor and one leg will usually be used for supporting the body and kick movement. The working leg makes the visual picture of a circular leg movement in front of the body. The working leg will start from one side and open up with an arc motion that finishes with the leg kick on the opposite side from where it started.

This same leg movement can be performed inward and outward. Flexibility in the hip rotation and strength of leg allow for a variation of adaptions when used in the choreography. It can be either a dynamic or a lyrical leg movement.

The Jazz Layout

Within jazz dance vocabulary, the layout is an exciting dance movement that is associated with, and part of, the kick family. The layout can produce a visual display of physical agility and control, yet requires a technical aptitude, as the whole body needs to be engaged to hit the mark.

Once again, the feeling of extension comes into its own in the layout position and should be used to support the body, so as not to add strain to the back. Using the plié on the supporting leg helps to cushion and support the spine, allowing the body to have an anchor to the ground to hold and sustain the kick and body extension position.

Gede Foster in the position of an off-balance jazz kick, using the relevé foot and lyrical sense of jazz dance movement. SIMON RICHARDSON

Final position of the outward round kick.

The layout can be an intimidating dance position for many dancers to execute, as it requires a fearless approach. Flexibility and core strength in the body are paramount. The feeling of extending out through the arms and legs allows this exciting jazz dance position to work to great effect in dance. As a movement, the layout can be used to enhance the choreographic approach and aptitude of the dancers. It can be a movement that can hit a single beat in the music or used in lyrical jazz dance as a slow extension and release with the leg.

Tilted Jazz Kicks

The tilted kicks are very much dependent on the flexibility or fearlessness of the dancer. The visual display and appearance of the tilt kick comes to life through the execution within the dance. The whole body is used to perform this exciting kick. Finding the technique to sustain the movement with the physical body needs care and thought. The placement of the kick is dependent on the dancer's physical ability. There is a feeling of extension through the

Samantha Tan in lyrical layout position.

SIMON RICHARDSON

Showing the jazz layout position.

Young jazz students practising an off-balance jazz kick with extension.

Dancers in class situation finding and attuning the alignment and balance for the position of an open tilt kick.

leg that is in the kick position and a strong supporting leg. The alignment of the body can be found by extending the energy through and out of the lower arm. Like most kicks that can be used in jazz dance, the tilt kick can be interpreted in varying ways, as shown in the images.

Hop, Skip and Jump Into Action

The explosion of differing styles of jumps, jetés and elevated movement, brings another attribute of dance movement and vocabulary to jazz dance. The use of elevation in jazz dance is an inherent strand of the physical dexterity of movement that is rooted within the kinetic and aesthetic jazz expression.

Dollie Henry striking a tilt kick. SIMON RICHARDSON

Preparation jump exercises – spring jumps from one foot to the other.

For a dancer at the beginning stages of their jazz dance training, understanding the energy and power needed to elevate the body off the floor is the first step. Simple jump exercises across the floor can assist a dancer to find timing, body position and stamina. The body cannot be expected to fly through the air without adequate preparation. It is through creating a solid footing and use of the floor that propels the movement and sustains the buoyancy of a jump and the flight of a jeté.

A suggested way to get going is with simple spring jumps from one foot to the other, in time with the music. To assist timing, using African drum music or jazz music derivatives that hold a musical reference that indicates a clear down beat can assist the dancer in finding their rhythm, timing and breathing control. This drives the footwork and energy required to support the dancer to elevate and land back to the floor in time.

Jumps can be practised as part of technique exercises, to build the dancer's agility, stamina, power and speed of movement. The practice of finding a solid dance technique will equip a dancer to find their own talent for flying through the air with ease and proficiency.

For the more advanced jazz class and dancer, creating jazz dance exercises across the floor can be enhanced by adding a combination of technical steps that includes an elevated movement or specific stylized jump. Jazz dance is noted for using an array of jumps and jetés, adding yet another layer to the visual and physical articulation of the jazz dance kinetic and aesthetic.

Examples of Jazz Jetés and Jumps

The movement, timing and power to execute a jeté/jump is interpreted by the style of dance and the aptitude of the dancer to deliver. The word jeté derives from the classical dance terminology meaning to throw or throwing and can be delivered in a number of ways in jazz dance.

Preparation jump exercise in second position.

A classic jazz jeté in motion.

Jeté placed and executed in second position facing front.

Position of an attitude stag jump in flight.

There are variations of a split jump – the legs can cross split or stay open in flight of movement.

Jumps and jetés require a solid and focused preparation to direct the energy, dynamics and dexterity of the body to propel off the floor into the air and descend with control and agility. The physical body must be warmed-up, and willing and able to experiment and adapt, as needed.

Variation on a tucked jump sometimes called a frog jump.

Variation on a split jump.

CHAPTER 7

A JAZZ DANCE EXERCISE PROGRAMME FOR THE MODERN-DAY JAZZ DANCER

AN OVERVIEW – TRAINING AND PREPARATION FOR THE JAZZ DANCER

As previously discussed, the jazz idiom is fundamentally an oral tradition passed down from artist to artist. This has resulted in only a limited number of practical guides produced that explain and analyse the numerous techniques and exercises that are a necessary part of the jazz dance tradition and its ongoing development.

Technical books that have been published have generally been written by a generation of jazz practitioners, many of whom are sadly no longer with us; for example, the Matt Mattox, Luigi and Giordano methods. Traditionally, jazz dance techniques and exercises are developed and shared by practitioners and choreographers who specialize in, and have an expertise of, the jazz dance form. The primary reason for this is to enable the dancer to develop a physical facility that enables them to artistically and technically express the creative work of the choreographer or teacher. In truth, all creative jazz dance practitioners and artists, including myself, aim to set new trends and develop a philosophy that references their specific style, technique, choreographic manifestation and deliverance of their particular jazz dance expression.

More recently, commercial trends in jazz dance have been the main motivation for many younger jazz teachers, where the focus is on learning dance steps and combinations, rather than a definable jazz

OPPOSITE: **The feet of a jazz performer.**

Dollie Henry showing the dance students the position of a stylized jazz jump to be executed in the choreography.

Dancers in the creative dance process, finding the shape and extension in the body through the dance movement.

Finding the individual expression, balance and connection to the movement of dance as shown in the position of a jazz layout.

technique. The body may be warm, but is it ready to dance? Is the dancer developing the physicality and mental aptitude to become a more accomplished jazz dancer?

To achieve a sustainable dance career, it is imperative that a dancer develops a strong and flexible body fit for executing the dance and skill to perform. This can only be achieved by regular and effective dance training. As a dancer, our main resource is our body; therefore, we have to respect our own physicality and look to refine our ability, skills and techniques through immersive and relevant practical jazz dance study.

Finding a Deeper Connection to Exercising

As with any form of dance, attaining a great dance technique alone will not make a great dancer. How we think also has an effect on how we dance. A thinking dancer is a dancer who can creatively engage and connect. A positive state of harmony between the body (physical) and the mind (emotional) can be created if we find a way to tap into, and connect to, our higher self.

Effective and appropriate dance training of any kind should seek to develop the whole creative spirit, offering the dancer an opportunity to balance and align the mind and the body. In this way, we create a conduit connecting our own personal creative truth with our individual jazz dance expression.

EXPLORING THE METHODOLOGY BEHIND JAZZ DANCE EXERCISES

Acquiring and sustaining a regular dance exercise and technique routine is vital for the dancer at the beginning of their dance life and should be an ongoing part of the professional dancer's physical development and artistic lifestyle.

The methodology outlined here was devised and developed after I suffered a severe hamstring injury some twenty-plus years ago. I created a sequence of jazz dance exercises and techniques that became an aid to my own physical recovery and assisted in retraining and reconditioning my physical body, and rewiring my mental and emotional intellect. The exercises and structure of my jazz dance class is focused on correctly attuning and developing muscular development, power and endurance, core strength and all-round body flexibility.

We are all aware of the importance of having the necessary physical tools and skills to be a proficient dancer, but often we forget about the mental aptitude needed to support that journey. The philosophy behind all I deliver through my jazz dance method is to fully equip and prepare the dancer's body and mind for performance. Often the mind can be the very reason we struggle to find that centred connection. My exercises are not only designed just to perfect technique, but also to unlock and free the creative mind.

My jazz dance exercise programme combines the techniques of jazz and classical dance with the added influences of more holistic exercises taken from yoga and pilates. The intention behind each exercise is not just to develop a honed physical body and technique, but, more importantly, to develop a physicality and mentality appropriate for jazz dance.

Keeping the body in tip-top condition takes work. The body is the conduit through which the embodiment of movement and dance will manifest.

Let the Music Lead the Way

Musicality and timing is everything. The music, specifically jazz music, plays an integral part and should form the soundscape for all jazz dance classes. The movement of jazz dance is formed within the movement when we exercise. It is the music that dictates the movement, dynamics, flow and demonstration of each exercise. The energy and response of movement behind every exercise is driven by the pulse of the music, which creates another level of connection for the dancer.

Dancers in time with the essence of the music bringing the movement and sound together.

IN THEIR OWN WORDS...

When the music changes, so does the dance.

African proverb

It is important to realize that the technique and the dance are not separated but coexist as one. Many dancers separate themselves from the music, often working through the exercises, out-of-time, forcing the movements and straining the body. Of course, intensive focus when exercising should be part of the acquisition of effective technique, but we are dancers and not circuit-training fanatics. The process of training and finding the movement and technique does not have to be so rigid or stifled.

Always dance with, and to, the music. Dance through your warm-up exercises, dance through your technical exercises, dance throughout your rehearsals, just dance, because that is what we are – dancers. Active and detailed listening to the music when you exercise will further develop your overall aural ability, so that you can quickly assimilate the

Every part of our body even in exercise should dance.

Jazz student dancers finding their own freedom of movement engaging as a community through the practice of class improvisation.

sound you hear to the flow and movement of your body. In jazz, nothing is separated, everything is intrinsically and creatively connected.

Getting in the Creative Zone

The repetition and routine of exercising can often be tedious, more so if we are not in the correct frame of mind. Approaching all exercises creatively will help to focus and connect the mind. It is all about connecting to your inner-self or 'being in the moment'.

'Being in the moment' is a difficult place to find and equally difficult to express on paper. This is because we are trying to define an emotional and personal feeling and connection. It is not unlike the head space of meditation coupled with the alertness of an athlete.

It all begins with focused concentration and effective breathing. Focus on your body and feel every movement made through the exercises. Visualize the flow of your body, connect it with the flow of the music and regulate through your effective breathing.

Every movement or step performed through the exercise process should be practised with clarity and precision. You are always attempting to reach another level of physical and mental attainment. Our body develops over time along with muscle memory; as long as we have the correct mental approach, we will strengthen and improve all aspects of our physicality and in turn our ability to realize the dance.

The Breath of Life

Let us take a moment to talk about breathing – a natural function of the body that keeps us all alive. Yet, most dancers I witness when teaching, have a tendency to hold their breath and forget to effectively breathe.

We need to practise how to breathe correctly, as this stimulates the flow of blood through our muscles. When we breathe, we relax, increasing the flexibility of movement when stretching out in exercise. Our breath supports the energy, timing, dynamics and flow of the movement, sustaining and enhancing our stamina levels needed when we dance. Just like a musician who has to blow their instrument, if they run out of breath, the musical notes will simply not escape.

Commitment

As with any dance training and exercise method, the dancer has to be ready to commit. Training the body

Marite Querel engaged in feeling her individual freedom of movement.

Melvin LeBlanc in the moment of finding his expression of movement.

and finding the technique of exercising can be a challenge. Step by step is the dancer's way, mastering any jazz dance exercise routine and technique is a process. The mind and the body require time to assimilate and understand the physicality of the movement you are developing. Be patient and give yourself time, as the jazz dance aesthetic requires great physical awareness and physical agility. Eventually, through committed training, your exercise regime and technique will be your conduit to achieving excellence in your dance performances.

Finally, feeling connected, free of tension and ready to interact openly and creatively is the ultimate goal. By correctly attuning the body, developing a strong jazz dance aesthetic and technique, we are setting ourselves free from the limitations of our dance physicality to truly express ourselves within the jazz dance tradition. It's all about switching on and finding your own creative space.

A SIMPLIFIED BREAKDOWN OF THE BOP JAZZ WARM-UP AND EXERCISES

When compiling this practical guide, my aim was that we identify and explain an effective and appropriate method of training for the jazz dancer. The obvious difficulty is that much of what we do as dancers is in the physical realm. In most circumstances, the best way to learn and acquire practical experience is by attending recognized jazz dance classes and workshops.

Jazz dance classes, techniques and exercises, are not confined to any one style or formula. Jazz practitioners and dance teachers will more often deliver their own approach and form of jazz dance, which will be aligned to the individual experience, ability as a dancer/teacher and comprehension, aesthetics, skills and techniques associated with jazz dance.

Over the last twenty years, my own particular jazz dance aesthetic and dance style define the delivery and method of my teaching practices. The warm-up exercises and the methodology described in this book sets the foundations for the technical and physical development of myself and that of my company dancers. This sets the premise of all my jazz classes in dance education within many performing arts colleges, universities, dance lectures and workshops, residencies and open jazz classes. However, the guiding influence behind my individual jazz expression and technique is very much informed by the African lineage and music traditions rooted within the jazz idiom.

As this book deals with static images, included is a visual guide with a variety of appropriate images that show the body positions practised and an explanation of the exercises that form the foundation of my jazz dance warm-up and physical development.

The programme method is a 45-minute warm-up and exercise class that is divided into six individual sections. Each section contains a series of condi-

Getting in the zone, finding a sense of balance and composure jazz meditation.

Dancers engaged and preparing the body and mind in a jazz warm-up.

tioning and strengthening exercises, stretches and dance movements that are devised to increase the blood flow, warming up the body from the inside to take the energy outward. Each section focuses on conditioning the body, whilst attaining and building strength, power, flexibility, alignment and core strength, control, coordination and musical timing.

Exercising correctly will assist the muscles to engage, building the physical muscular endurance and power within the body. Flexibility exercises support the muscles and increase the elasticity of movement. Core development aids the dynamic energy and power from the centre of the body. Breathing focuses and settles the mind, whilst building the cardiovascular levels that feed the muscles and assists in developing the required stamina to eventually execute the dance.

Music plays a significant part in the process of my own jazz warm-up exercises, technical floor exercises and the resulting class choreography. It is from the connection to the music that a natural jazz technique is able to develop, that of musical timing and aural awareness. The music (jazz music) guides the natural ebb and flow, dynamics and impulse of movement and natural coordination, creating a real sense of connectivity to the dance within the exercises.

A Breakdown of Each Section of Exercise

- Section One: pre-warm-up.
- Section Two: pliés, relevés, lunges and leg stretches.
- Section Three: head and shoulders, isolations and upper body exercises.
- Section Four: feet, legs and kick exercises, concluding with a series of jump exercises.
- Section Five: floor exercises, including intensive stretching, abdominal and core exercises.
- Section Six: the cool down.

Getting Started

For a jazz dance class, unlike ballet, the warm-up and exercises are practised without the barre, set and practised as centre work. The only assistance and resistance the dancer has is the floor, and that dance floor has to become the dancer's best friend and support.

To enable this connection to the floor, I prefer to have bare or socked feet (meaning, no shoes) when exercising. This allows a sense of freedom, so that the feet can really connect to the floor within the warm-up and stretch, without hindrance.

Connecting with yourself and your space is very important when we dance. Plugging into a non-

Strong and secure placement and position of the body gives a feeling of being rooted to the dance floor, in the same way we can imagine a tree is rooted to the earth.

visible source of energy takes some creative and open-minded thinking. I have always viewed the body as a human reflection of the jazz tree, rooting itself to the earth and using the energy for growth and expansion of its branches.

Always take a moment before you start any exercise to place your body in the correct physical and mental position. If you imagine, and then feel, that the central line through the body is like a spiral that works up from the floor through your body (core) and exits at the top of your head, you are already connecting with your inner self. Always make sure the body weight is distributed evenly between both feet. The upper body should be centrally positioned, your weight slightly forward towards your toes and not sitting back into the heels of the feet.

Section One: The Pre-Warm-Up

The pre-warm is devised to allow the dancer to find their own energy within the studio space – what I like to call 'getting into the zone': that moment of being able to switch off from the everyday pressures of normal life and to have the chance to place yourself in that physical and mental frame of mind is important to find. The body and mind needs a moment of time to prepare for the more physical and technical exercises that will follow within the class.

The pre-warm-up gives the body a chance to awaken, reducing and hopefully preventing any unwanted injury and damage to the muscles and ligaments. Using the pre-warm-up gives yet another chance to settle and adjust the breathing so allowing a chance to engage from within, which in return will allow the movements to flow more easily, so that when exercising or dancing, effective breathing becomes second nature.

The pre-warm-up is also a chance to set free the natural endorphins that produce that natural high and boost the feeling of energy and positivity within the body.

A variation of technical exercises and stretches used in Section One:

- Shoulder rolls
- Body stretch and releases against the legs
- Glute and hamstring stretches
- Upper body, shoulder and arm stretches
- Variety of side and rib stretches
- Flat back position and flat back to floor
- Stretches for the back of the legs

Shoulder rolls practised using the plié for gentle bounce in motion with shoulder rolls.

Body release and stretch against legs on diagonal.

Body and leg stretch to the front.

Deep plié glute stretch.

Upper body and shoulder stretch using the plié.

Side and rib stretch variation.

Side stretch variation.

Flat back to horizontal position.

Flat back position to the floor.

Section Two: Pliés, Relevés, Lunges and Leg Stretches

The Plié

My own style of jazz dance is informed by the use of the plié. My exercises, therefore, home in on developing the plié as it enables the physicality of the movement to stay and to feel grounded and connected to the floor. It is a transferable skill essential for speed, jumps, power and the agility of dance movement.

Within training, the plié strengthens the legs and muscles, and serves as a physical exercise for turn out in the hips. It opens up the glute (buttocks) muscles to release tension, so aiding further flexibility, and provides more power in the lower body.

The use of the plié is a natural technique and skill when applied in jazz dance as it directly links to the aesthetic of the jazz dance form.

TOP LEFT: **Full plié in first position.**

TOP RIGHT: **Full plié in second position with arms.**

Dancers executing the full plié in first position in jazz warm-up.

I remind all my students to pay attention to the placement and position of the plié in exercise, making sure not to release the tail bone but to keep it tucked under, and making sure you align your body centrally through the plié movement. This strengthens the pelvic floor, whilst increasing the central core power and strength that is essential for control and flexibility of physical movement for jazz dance.

The Relevé or Rise

Although the relevé is often associated with ballet, it is also used in jazz for building strength in the ankles, calves, thighs, glutes and core. As we dance with our feet, they need to be warm and supple, yet strong and powerful to carry the dance movement. Adding specific relevé exercises within the warm-up encourages the dancer to also focus on balance and alignment of the body.

Dancers executing full plié in second position in jazz warm-up.

Plié in second position with relevé, which assists in strengthening the ankles, legs, glutes and core body and development of balance.

Relevé or rise in second position.

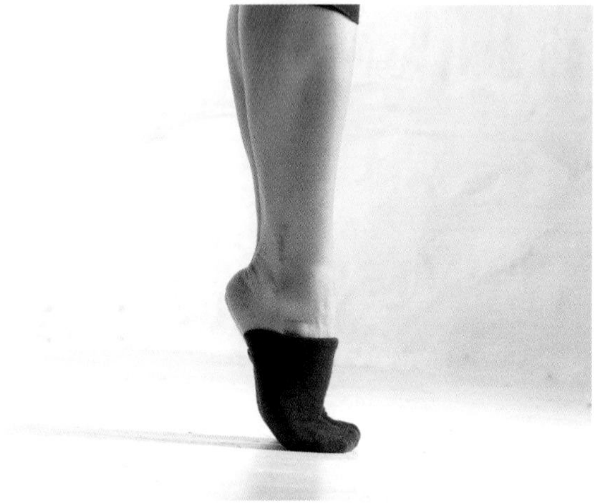

Relevé or rise in parallel position from the side.

Using the relevé/rise in action.

Lunges and Leg Stretches

These are practised to stretch deep in to the frontal hip muscles, glutes and back of the legs. The exercises are intended to create a feeling of extension of leg movement and to develop flexibility. These exercises will also help to sculpture and tone the muscles of the legs, hips and glutes.

Lunge position 1.

Lunge position 2, adding upper body spiral stretch.

Section Three: Head, Neck and Upper Body Stretches and Exercises

This section of exercises works on releasing, stretching and strengthening the upper body. The exercises aim to loosen and engage the muscles and movement of the head and neck, working through to the shoulders, the spine, into the ribs and hip isolations. The upper body is also given a good workout through engaging and developing the upper-body core muscles and assists the dancer in finding a physical connection to this part of the body.

Exercises used in Section Three:

- Neck stretch and shoulder release exercises
- Head rolls
- Shoulder rolls and circular arm swings
- Dynamic upper-body stretch and release exercises
- Rib and hip isolations exercises
- Flat back, contractions and balance exercises
- Core strengthening exercises

Hip and leg lunge stretch to second.

Upper body stretch and release.

MIDDLE LEFT: **Flat back position from the side. It is important to keep the weight forward into the toes so as to build core strength and balance, making sure to take the energy forward beyond the fingertips.**

BOTTOM LEFT: **Flat back exercise for balance incorporating the rise for further balance and core control.**

BOTTOM RIGHT: **Upper body side stretch. This full body stretch opens the ribs and also acts as a movement of release.**

Section Four: Feet, Ankles, Full Leg and Kick Exercises Concluding with Jumps

For the jazz dancer, attaining strong feet and legs is paramount. I use a combination of foot exercises that work through the whole foot right to the end of your toes, with the addition of further relevés, tendu and fondu exercises. The leg exercises continue through with thigh stretches and kicks, culminating with a round of jumps. These exercises will strengthen, tone and lengthen the muscles through control of movement and flow, helping to develop strong, defined and powerful leg movements.

As much of these exercises are placed in the centre of the studio floor without the use of a ballet barre, there is a greater demand on the body and balance. The exercises assist in the development of a stronger core control, which in turn enhances the ability of balance and alignment through the central line and upper body carriage.

Exercises used in Section Four:

Foot pedal exercises.

- Foot pedals exercises
- Hamstring/back of leg stretches
- Relevé exercises to strengthen ankles and attaining core balance
- A series of tendu, fondu and leg extension exercises
- Variation of leg strengthening and extension exercises
- Thigh and frontal hip stretch exercises
- Kicks in attitude and grand battement positions – both delivered in central position or using pas de bourée, as the preparation dance step to deliver the movement of the kick
- Jumps exercised in differing foot positions for stamina and elevation

Foot pedal exercise in first position.

Back of leg stretch, hamstring and Achilles' stretch exercise.

Hamstring, back of leg and full body flexibility stretch. These exercises are not to be forced, breathing through the stretch and lengthening the body develops flexibility.

Full body and back of leg stretch with feet placed in parallel position. Imagine that the body is making the perfect V shape.

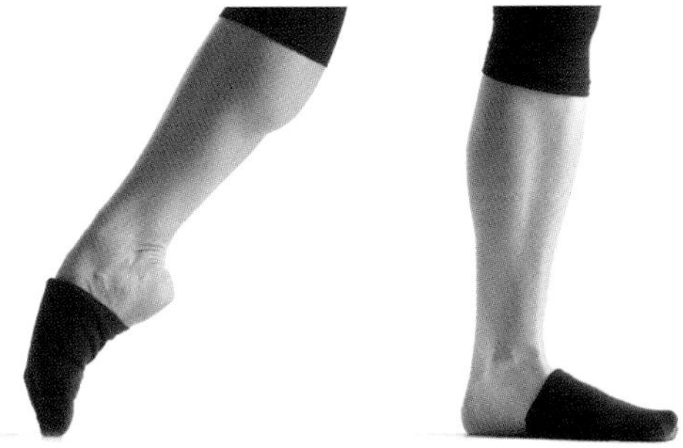

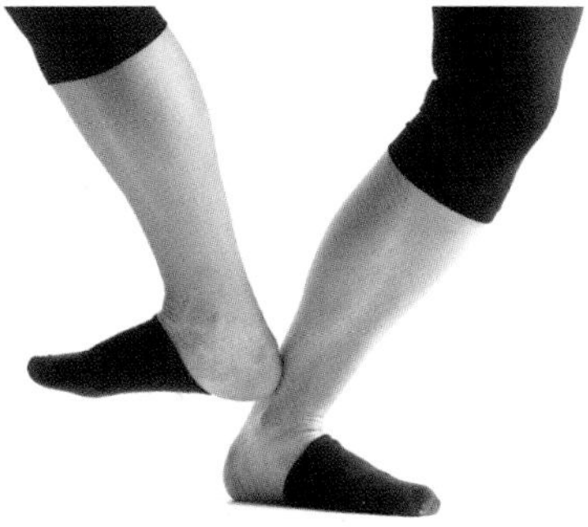

TOP LEFT: **The rise is used to assist control in the ankles, core strength and balance.**

TOP RIGHT: **Advanced balance on the rise with arms in parallel position.**

MIDDLE LEFT: **Tendu to second position.**

MIDDLE RIGHT: **Fondu position in the leg exercises.**

BOTTOM RIGHT: **Exercise with extended leg with flexed foot.**

Leg balance in open attitude placed in second position.

Développé leg exercise to second position – this is also practised to the front and back positions.

Leg and thigh stretch 1.

Thigh and hip stretch 2.

Battement kick with straight leg to second position.

Side view of battement kick with straight leg.

Dollie Henry performing a spontaneous and exciting jazz kick.

Section Five: Floor Exercises

By this point in the exercise process, the body should be sufficiently and adequately warmed-up to have produced a healthy glow or sweat. Now it's time to hit the floor.

Through this section, the concentration is on intensive stretching, toning and strengthening, paying attention to the whole body, but in particular the legs and the upper and lower abdominal and pelvic muscles.

Exercising from the floor.

Forward spine stretch over legs. This exercise stretches and releases the lower back, glute and hips.

Exercises used in Section Five:

- Upper body and spinal stretches
- Upper body spiral stretch
- Variation of hip, leg flex and release exercises and stretches
- Hips, inner thigh and box split stretches
- Further intensive flexibility glute, hamstring and leg stretches
- Core contraction and release exercises

Full extension stretch over legs viewed from the front.

Lengthened spinal stretch. Taking energy from the base of the spine right through to the top of the head.

Curved or contracted spinal stretch position.

Full spiral stretch position.

Frog position for opening the hips and inner thighs.

Leg and body stretch with flexed feet.

Full body release and forward stretch over legs.

Box split with side stretch 1.

Box split over the leg stretch 2.

Forward stretch in second position.

Beginning of contraction and release exercises.

Finish position of contraction and release exercises.

Abdominal/Core Strength Exercises

Attaining receptive abdominal muscles and core strength is vital for the dancer. The core of the body is the central anchor point for all our dance movements. This series of exercises helps to develop the upper and lower abdominal muscles. Strong abdominals influence your posture, poise and physical power, and makes for a more toned, physical look for any dancer. It is not just about achieving that amazing six pack, but more about achieving that core power that enhances the physical ability and the dynamic forces required for the dance and movement.

Exercises used:

- A variation of abdominal crunch and power sit-ups
- Deep core coccyx balance exercises
- Lower abdominal power resistance exercises
- Press-ups and plank exercises

Abdominal crunch exercise.

Coccyx sit-up with knees bent at right angle.

Coccyx sit-up with straight legs.

Pelvic floor resistance exercises.

Plank position.

Press-up from the knee position.

Full leg press-up position.

Hip and Hamstring Stretches and Flexibility Stretch Exercises

The final section of the warm-up is focused on exercises that assist the legs and hips to find a deeper flexibility and extension throughout. The aim is to destress and release the muscles. These exercises require a sense of fluidity, which is aided by correct breathing with the movement throughout the exercises.

Kick exercises allow the energy to be released through the entire leg and helps build and assist the dynamic of movement and use of resistance, which also helps to tone the muscles and develop more strength and power in the legs.

Exercises used:

- Hamstring, thigh and back of leg stretches
- Hip and pelvic stretch (spider stretch)
- Lower spine stretch and release exercise
- Series of resistance kick exercises with pointed and flexed foot

Hamstring and thigh stretch to align the body and hips.

Hamstring and leg resistance.

Full leg-release and flexibility stretch.

Hip and pelvic release (spider stretch).

ABOVE: **Floor kick with pointed foot.**

Floor kick with flexed foot.

Section Six: The Cooling Down Process

This is the moment to regulate breathing and heartbeat, and for taking a moment to feel the energy of the body. Cooling down is exactly that, through a series of gentle stretches. The body should be sufficiently warmed-up and engaged physically and mentally to begin the next process of jazz dance training that focuses on practical and technical dance exercises across the floor.

RIGHT: **Cool down – side stretch.**

Cool down – full body release.

Floor cool down – lower spine stretch.

Floor cool down – shoulder and chest stretch.

Practising across the floor split jetés.

A General Note

Endless repetition in class can stunt the dancers' growth and bring complacency to the purpose of training and exercising. I make it a rule to keep the delivery of my jazz exercise class as fresh and spontaneous as possible by occasionally varying the exercise routine. The structure of a jazz dance class warm-up can be adapted by adding new exercises and techniques when and if needed, as can the accompanying music. A successful exercise programme will always adapt to the needs of the dancer, improving their weaknesses and developing their strengths. This keeps the dancer on their toes (literally), keeping the mind focused and connected. The unseen technique of jazz dance is to always attempt to be in the moment, even when in exercise mode. Equally important is that feel-good factor. By the end of the warm-up, the body should have a rush of endorphins that can be channelled into the dance.

THE PURPOSE OF 'OPEN FLOOR' TECHNICAL DANCE EXERCISES

I like to think of this part of the jazz class as the pre-dance moment. The exercises and warm-up serve to awaken the body, prepare and tune the muscles and to create a connection between the movement and music. The next stage of the class is to guide the dancer to further engage in the creative process for perfecting the jazz dance skills and techniques that will be required for realizing jazz choreography.

Dance floor exercises form an important line of practice within a concise technical jazz dance class. There is a journey that the dancer needs to go on in order to build upon the techniques and exercises after the physical warm-up. As the warm-up exercises are practised in a fairly static situation, the dancer needs to find a real sense of dance movement through applying a combination of jazz dance steps as technical dance sequences.

Dance Floor Exercises: Developing Jazz Steps and Combinations

Dance floor exercises provide an opportunity for the

dancer to become familiar, through practice, with the jazz dance vocabulary, jazz steps and combinations.

To understand the nature of jazz dance movement is to understand the purpose of the steps and how they can be used in the resulting jazz choreography. The music has a great influence on how we move, as each step is defined by the pulse, timing, syncopation and dynamics of the music.

Dance floor exercises and step combinations can easily be adapted to suit the level of the dancer or the jazz dance skill that needs to be worked upon. Simple exercises that combine walks, turns, kicks and jumps assist the dancer with weight distribution, fluidity of movement, musical timing, dynamics, spatial and directional awareness. As the dancer progresses, more advanced steps and combinations can be created that require more technique and flexibility; for example, combining pas de bourées, pirouettes, jazz layouts and variations on a jeté. The aim is to challenge and stimulate the dancer to engage with the steps, as if learning a piece of choreography.

Practising the technique of jazz dance using the legs within the jazz exercise combination.

Dancers developing their performance skills as part of the process within the floor dance exercises.

CHAPTER 8

KEYNOTES FOR TEACHING JAZZ DANCE

THE JAZZ PRACTITIONER AND THE JAZZ DANCE TEACHER

Jazz dance practitioners and jazz dance teachers are placed in that unique position of creative responsibility as mentors. A competent teacher can change the lives and direct many young children, students and professional dancers in unlocking and achieving their potential as jazz dancers.

Often young dance students are required to learn a set jazz dance syllabus, set out by examination boards for grading and assessing the dancer's development. The examination format dictates to the teacher how to set and structure the said technique for jazz dance.

When the student dancer moves on to performance college, other forms and styles of jazz techniques, which relate to the college academic structure, are taught by individual jazz teachers/practitioners within the educational establishment.

Outside of the educational situation are the open studio jazz classes that provide a platform for teachers and creative dance practitioners to achieve an identification of their individual expression and, more importantly, a technique and creative example that is related to their personal style and expression.

As dance teachers, we are engaged with a visual art form and the ability to 'show' in a class or creative situation is essential. Jazz dance emulates our own vision and experiences. It is our own body and ability that becomes our primary resource for

IN THEIR OWN WORDS...

I am a dance teacher... I am thankful for the opportunity to pass on my passion for the art of dance.

Rhee Gold

OPPOSITE: Dollie Henry teaching and demonstrating a jazz layout with dancers from Menchu Duran Escola Dansa Summer Residency 2016, Barcelona.

RIGHT: Dollie Henry teaching and sharing with a young group of Spanish dancers in a jazz dance workshop.

Dance students in the creative process finding their own personal expression.

the student to become inspired, enlightened and mentored.

As jazz dance is from the aural and improvised expression, it is imperative for the dance teacher to be at the top of their own game, knowledgeable in the dance style, with a clear knowledge of the core aesthetic and vocabulary of movements that identify the core expression and delivery of the jazz dance form. To be connected when we teach dance is more than just sharing a sequence of steps lifted from the page, grabbed from YouTube or borrowed from a favourite music video or musical theatre production.

The inclusivity of the jazz idiom allows for a great variety of teaching approaches and creative outcomes for teaching jazz dance. How we teach is dependent on our own personal and individual approach, our own experiences, comprehensive understanding and knowledge of the dance form we aim to pass on.

It is important that as a teacher we continue to train and develop our own individual creative expression, so that we can encourage, support and mentor our dance students to find their own individual creative expression and real joy of jazz dance.

Here are some simple tips for staying informed, current and creatively inspired:

- Give time to research and become more informed on the history of jazz dance. Inspiration comes in many forms.
- As our dancers grow, so should we. Remember to refresh and update your jazz class structure, adapting and building the skillset to your exercises and dance combinations.
- Deepen your musical knowledge. Spend some time searching out differing styles of jazz music and related musical derivatives. Jazz music has a unique energy and vibration that supports the physical, emotional and aural senses.

- Engage in, and observe, professional jazz choreographers' practice of the art form. They all have something to draw from that can inform your own method of teaching and choreographic outcomes.
- Define and continue to develop your own jazz technique and individual practice of teaching.
- Stay inspired, inquisitive and innovative. Don't forget to experiment and explore your own creative journey as a teacher. As we teach, we are also in a situation of growth and learning – it works both ways.

THE SKILL OF IMPROVISATION

Improvisation is a significant strand that provides jazz with its unique creative delivery and initial choreographic outcomes. There are some dance teachers and dancers who find improvising in a class situation daunting. There is no need for fear, as the truth is, we improvise every day. When we meet someone for the first time, we are improvising; when we are writing, we improvise the words to form the message. In reality, improvisation is at the core of everything we do in life. In artistic terms, I like to think of improvisation in dance as a creative freedom of expression:

- For the jazz teacher, it is through understanding the processes of improvisation that an individual confidence is built and individual dance style can be developed.
- For the jazz dance creator, improvisation is the process through which to find the freedom to explore yourself creatively and to develop your dance works.
- For the jazz dancer, improvisation is a necessary tool and creative skill, which can be used to great effect, both in rehearsals and the performance situation.

Let's not be mistaken, improvising is not a matter of creating random dance movements, tricks and steps that have no connection to the music, aesthetic style and specific dance technique. Quite the opposite, there is depth and intelligence to improvising that inspires and encourages the jazz exponent to find a deeper connection, greater confidence and individual jazz dance language that is connected to the music narrative.

The practice and development for a jazz dancer should be no different from that of the jazz musician. When observing and listening to jazz musicians, aside of knowing the scale, melody and musical changes, much that is performed is from improvi-

Emmanuella Idris captured whilst improvising during a rehearsal session. Spontaneous moments often make for interesting photographic compositions.

sational practice and delivery. The jazz musician, when performing solo moments within a performance, shares within the overall ensemble sound, yet has the open space to add their own personal expression in the moment. Nothing preconceived, just spontaneous at the point of play. Jazz dance offers a similar arc of creativity, the freedom to express as an individual performer and yet still be in synchronicity with the other dancers in the ensemble.

IN THEIR OWN WORDS...

The dance comes out of the music and the music out of the dance.

Dollie Henry

Improvisation and the Jazz Dance Teacher

For any dance teacher following the traditions of the jazz expression, improvisation is an essential skill to acquire and develop. Understandably, there are differing demands placed upon the jazz dance teacher, depending on the teaching situation, level and structure of the jazz class. For jazz teachers of open classes, it is not always possible or practical to implement a jazz dance class based solely on improvisation. Therefore, it is not unusual in these teaching situations to have a number of prepared motifs and combinations to base your class choreography on. However, what is important is how you derived these initial ideas. As jazz creators, they should stem from our interpretations of the music; therefore, we need to originate our ideas for our improvisations in the dance studio. The improvisatory element within the actual class will stem from

Dollie Henry and dancers in a creative session – keeping dancers engaged is part of the creative process.

Martina Farkasova and Melvin Le Blanc improvising upon ideas developed in rehearsals.

the order in which we use these initial ideas and the links between the set combinations.

For the teacher of jazz dance in performing arts' establishments, there is the opportunity to develop creative improvisation, along with the process and technique, over a longer time frame. Obviously, we all need to be confident in our individual abilities as dance teachers to improvise, as we need to be able to show students our creative dance ideas. It also follows that our warm-ups, technical and skill-based exercises are fundamental to the success of our class-based improvisation.

As experienced dance teachers, our bank of creative ideas is the springboard from which our ideas for improvisation originate. How we creatively 'frame' our improvisation development in the dance class depends on the structure and style of both the music and resulting dance.

Personally, for the more advanced jazz class or jazz workshop, I like to challenge my own jazz 'chops' with a blank canvas. As often as possible I like to create in the moment, improvising all my ideas as I respond to the music. Music is the source for accessing all my initial ideas for creating dance. I use the music as the sounding board for the specific jazz dance style and narrative that will eventually be used as the focus point of my choreography. Although this 'high-wire' style of teaching can be somewhat daunting, it keeps me attached to the true essence of the jazz idiom. No prepared choreography, nothing preconceived, just the chosen music, myself and my dance students, engaged together on a creative jazz dance journey. The secret is to be aurally connected and immerse yourself in the music you will be using for your dance class. Listen to the detail of the musical score, the stylistic concept, the instrumental interplay, the groove and syncopation, musical highs and lows and flow of the music. Let all your creative senses absorb the sound, as it is the music that always inspires the dance movement and improvisation, so creating dance that is unique and in the moment.

Building the confidence and becoming more comfortable and flexible in the ability to improvise, opens another world for the jazz teacher. Tapping into our creative channels assists in finding our own truth and individual expression.

Improvisation and the Jazz Choreographer

For the jazz choreographer, improvisation should be at the root of all jazz dance creations. Within a company environment, effective warm-ups, technical exercises and stylistic combinations would be practised regularly. Consequently, a jazz vocabulary and effective stylistic understanding would be in place. In keeping with the process of jazz dance improvisation, the dance would be created in the studio with the company. It is imperative that dancers have excellent retention skills, so they can 'capture' the initial improvisatory ideas. These initial ideas are further refined through repetition. Often individuals in the company will continue a movement or interpret your improvisations differently. These moments are also important to consider and develop, if necessary. There is an important collaborative nature creating jazz dance in this manner. Your eyes, as a choreographer, are essential here, as you seek to adapt fleeting improvisations into more substantial movements and combinations. Retain (and record) everything, as it is about being in the moment and embracing the inclusivity of jazz.

Nothing is wasted; improvisational ideas can be stored in the choreographic bank to draw from at a later stage and can provide the source of inspiration to commencing the process for developing and creating your original jazz dance masterpieces. A choreographer working with dancers to create through improvisation enables a collective experience and develops an artistic unity that will follow through into performance. It also supports the dancers to refine their individual interpretations and allows the chorographer to work with dancers' individual techniques and dance physicality. Over time, through improvisation a company will develop an artistic cohesion and collective stylistic approach that enables high artistic dance creations.

Jazz dance improvisation in performance is exhilarating, exciting and challenging in equal measure. Success with performance improvisation is very much aligned to the experience and intuitive ability of the dancer. There is, obviously, creative freedom when improvising, but it must be relevant to both the music and the style of the dance you are creating. If the company of dancers are well versed in improvisatory technique and have a clear sense of the company style, improvisation in performance is an enriching and creatively rewarding experience both for the performer and the audience.

Creating and developing a jazz dance through improvisation using the dancers and props to create the visual setting.

Improvisation and the Jazz Dancer

The art of improvisation for the dancer is the ability to have the freedom to create movement that is instinctive and spontaneous and yet still shares the jazz dance aesthetic. For the dancer inexperienced in jazz improvisation, it is essential to mentor an understanding of both the process and technique of creative improvisation.

Developing and creating improvisational strategies in the rehearsal room and in dance classes will assist the choreographer and the dancer to consolidate and further develop their individual jazz dance aesthetic.

Initial improvisational exercises should always be led by the music. For example, choose a piece of jazz music that reflects the emotional or narrative content of your intended improvisation. Encourage your dancers to identify all the individual musical instruments heard, the basic tempo and essence of the music. Allocate each dancer an instrument or, better still, let them choose an instrument that resonates with them and encourage them to improvise initial movement to the musical sound. The experience and outcome for each dancer will be very different, depending on their dance vocabulary, and their technical and creative abilities. As the outside eye, you the teacher/choreographer can support your dancers to connect more closely with the direction of the music, and to develop and adapt their movements through effective analysis of the improvisations. As you further develop these improvisational exercises, for either a solo or dance ensemble, you can refine ideas over time to be developed into future choreographic models and motifs.

In the long-term, improvisation techniques and skills will assist dancers to overcome their fears, to explore their own narrative dance voices, to take more creative risks, and to develop the emotional and mental capacities to dance and perform with a sense of freedom and confidence that expresses their individuality as jazz dancers.

Improvisation in performance is the jazz dancers' golden ticket for adjusting a mistake. Having the skill to improvise can also get a dancer out of trouble in the performance situation. The fear for any dancer is that horrendous possibility of going blank on stage or losing the dance steps in mid-flow of performance. In the worst-case scenario, improvisation can be the saving grace for a dancer who is confident in their ability to produce dance in the moment without hesitation. Improvisation is the art of being able to recover and continue on track as if nothing wrong ever happened.

Martina Farkasova performing *Olivers Twist* live jazz event with jazz guitarist Chris Standring, Cadogan Hall, London.

CHAPTER 9

CREATING DANCE FOR JAZZ THEATRE

BRINGING YOUR CREATIVE IDEAS TO LIFE

As jazz dance stems from initial improvisation, it is natural that many jazz dancers are inspired to develop their own choreography. Choreography demands a great deal from us as jazz dance creators. We need first-rate technique, great communication skills, musical appreciation, original creative ideas and also a reason for creating. Original jazz theatre productions, concert dance pieces and jazz music compositions that reflect and bring to life all that is of the jazz idiom are the motivation behind the choreography. For a teacher who is setting a dance to their students to the choreographer who looks to create a dance piece or narrative dance story, the concept and idea needs to be clear.

IN THEIR OWN WORDS...

The things you are passionate about are not random, they are your calling.

Fabienne Fredrickson

Most dance is notated, for example, by the Laban technique, which is used to preserve the steps and choreography in dance. This form of capturing and logging the dance is used much more in the ballet and the contemporary dance worlds. Some may find

OPPOSITE: **Dollie Henry performing *Aranjuez* from BOP production *Touches of Miles.***

BOP company performing the character-driven jazz theatre repertoire *Moods of the Night.*

BRENDON HANSFORD

it easier to notate their choreography as a reminder. Today, with technology at our hands, videoing the creative and rehearsal process enables a much easier way to log, review and edit the creative work. There are no specific rules, it is all about finding your own way to plan and form your creative jazz dance theatre masterpiece.

Creating Jazz Dance

This chapter seeks to demystify the creative process and share some tips and guides to new jazz teachers and dance creatives with a series of strategies and techniques that can be applied to assist the creative process.

The premise behind everything we produce for our dance company is to create original jazz theatre that reflects and artistically champions the jazz art form. Through our artistic company, BOP, we have been creating jazz theatre works for over twenty years. This has afforded us a comprehensive understanding of the processes and methods required to devise and develop original jazz theatre.

Creating is initially an individual expression that we then seek to express outwardly. Although we look to begin our creative work with an initial spark of inspiration, there are many practical techniques that we can learn and develop to assist in the creative exploration and realization of that initial idea.

Andrew Denton performing *Juba Jump* from BOP Jazz Theatre *Footprints in Jazz* (2013). BRENDON HANSFORD

Dollie Henry and Paul Jenkins performing *Fusion* from *Journey of Jazz*. WILLIAM POTTER

The starting point of any jazz choreographer's process of creating jazz dance is the ability and expression of one's own dance technique.

Your job as a dance creator is to develop your dance body to its fullest extent in order to give you the ability to show your creation with your own body. Jazz dance is passed on by what we see and what we hear, so as you create, it is essential that your dance technique can display that. All choreographers need like-minded and creative dancers through which to express their work. As a choreographer, your collaborative skills are essential to the success of your creative outcomes. For the jazz choreographer, our creative collaboration also extends to that with the music and/or composers. So the first part of your process as a jazz choreographer is the music.

Connecting to the Music

One of the great successes of jazz music is its diversity. Indeed, much of today's commercial music weaves its way back to jazz and many of us have danced to the beats of popular music in our jazz class. However, you will find it helpful to develop a practical appreciation of the different derivatives and styles of jazz music, thus developing an awareness of the many different sounds, rhythms and textures. Your chosen music needs to reflect your initial creative vision, so choose a piece of music that inspires the dance and movement in you.

To help us choose the music, we need to be aware of the movements that might initially be associated with the type of musical sound we are listening to. For example, if we were to listen to the pulsating rhythms of authentic swing jazz, we could be drawn to the form and narrative of the lindy-hop styles, which could be used as a template to inform the dance narrative. Conversely, inspiration could flow from the cool jazz sounds of Miles Davis, suggesting a more flowing and lyrical jazz approach, or to the sounds of Gregory Porter, for example, his recording of *Liquid Spirit* with its more contemporary rhythmic drive and gospel undertone. There are also the larger and grander jazz orchestrations and jazz works of composers such as Duke Ellington, Quincy Jones or Lalo Schifrin, or the more contemporary jazz sounds of Pat Metheny, Herbie Hancock and Terence Blanchard.

It is the music that helps dictate the movements and combinations that we create. Remember, listen to the music and understand the style and layers of rhythms and textures that can help you create your jazz work. There is always the underlying pulse; this is the heart beat of the music that will allow your movement to flow. Do not forget the intricate rhythms that are behind the main pulse. Then focus on the more melodic sounds, trace the melody in your mind's ear. Finally, consider the layering of the sounds, from very sparse to textually full.

Tapping into that Initial Creative Spark

The unique creative approach that all jazz artists share is that improvisation forms the basis of all our work. How that improvisation articulates itself creatively is dependent on the art form you are engaged in. For the jazz choreographer, the improvisatory approach is in a more structured way; the elements of improvisation occur both inside and outside of the dance studio. As you listen to the music, allow your creative mind to begin to visualize movements; often the very first idea is the hardest to find. Therefore, having a few ideas of dance movements and stylistic themes before the first rehearsal is a sensible approach.

There is always a balance to achieve when creating: how much is developed outside of the dance studio and how much through the rehearsal process. With both approaches, as an accomplished jazz dancer, you would have developed a foundation and practical understanding of different positions, movements, motifs and combinations that can act as your initial visual template from which to build. Remember, you already have a bank of ideas and techniques through your own dance experience. The trick is to organize and arrange these in a manner that is unique to you. Do not be afraid to experiment with your ideas, this is just the beginning. Structure and pace can be organized later, but allow your creative ideas to flow unabated. Work these initial ideas with your dancers and observe closely how they interpret your movements.

Valentina Dolci performing the lyrical jazz solo *Last Dance with My Father* from BOP Jazz Theatre.
WILLIAM POTTER

One of the great assets of the jazz idiom is that we seek a personal interpretation; the important creative resource is you and your dancers. Therefore, it is in the nature of creating jazz dance that adjustments will be made as your piece develops. It may be that one of your dancers may have a particular interpretation or technical ability that allows you to develop further your initial ideas. Previously, we discussed the notion of a collaborative approach, well here it is.

Developing the Work

Once you have begun the process of developing your dance piece, it is important that you review and consolidate your ideas. If we start our creation through improvisation, then it is helpful to record this and reflect on the work to date. You may find it appropriate to notate your choreography as a reminder. In my early days of creating, I developed my own version of choreographic notation with dots for the dancers and arrows to determine the direction of dancer. Today I video all the creative and rehearsal process to be able to review and edit, if needed.

As your work develops in the studio, you need to strike the right balance between your individual dancer's interpretation and your imagined physicality of the piece you are creating. You need to achieve the correct balance here as the work needs to reflect your personal jazz style, but with reference to your dancer's technical and performance abilities.

If you follow the above strategy your work should reflect your individuality through the movement you have created, responding to your chosen music. Each new piece we choreograph will enable us to further develop all aspects of our creative process, so it is important that we create as often as we can.

BOP company performing *Fusion*. SCOTT JORDANE

As with most art, our creating is very much dependent on our own individual bank of ideas and our experiences. Therefore, it is essential that we fill up our bank constantly by watching, listening and analysing the work of other choreographers and composers for inspiration and guidance.

Finally, creating can be a daunting and vulnerable place, especially as a choreographer, but we should not forget to enjoy the process. The reason why we all started to dance and develop our individual choreographic skills is because we have something to say about ourselves through the expression of dance.

IN THEIR OWN WORDS...

Making dances is an act of progress; it is an act of growth, an act of music, an act of teaching, an act of celebration, an act of joy.

Alvin Ailey

Dollie Henry and Remy Martyn performing *Freddie Freeloader* from the BOP Jazz Theatre production *Touches of Miles*. BRIAN APPIAH OBENG

Company dancers striking a stylized pose and motif in the contemporary BOP Jazz dance piece *Directions*.

BRIAN APPIAH OBENG

BOP dancers rehearsing for a music video.

THE CREATIVE JAZZ CAKE

I often put my thinking into sections and call it my 'creative cake'. Some practical concepts that I use, and I hope will assist you the dancer and teacher in finding your own creative process, are outlined below.

- Theme
- Music
- Structure
- Choreography
- Performers
- Costumes
- Lighting
- Stage

Theme of the Work

Starting any dance creation or developing repertoire can be particularly daunting, so preparation is all. Be sure to have a clear perception of your creative theme, narrative or image. The initial creating process starts from this point. You may already have an idea running through your mind. Just get those ideas out of your head and on to paper. You can add and delete the pages as the ideas develop through your process. Your theme can be as simple as responding to the beats of the music, to a fully developed expressive narrative such as Ailey's *Revelations*. If you are new to choreography, keep your themes clear and concise. Remember, one minute of creative choreography can take a full rehearsal session of between three and five hours, a five-minute piece

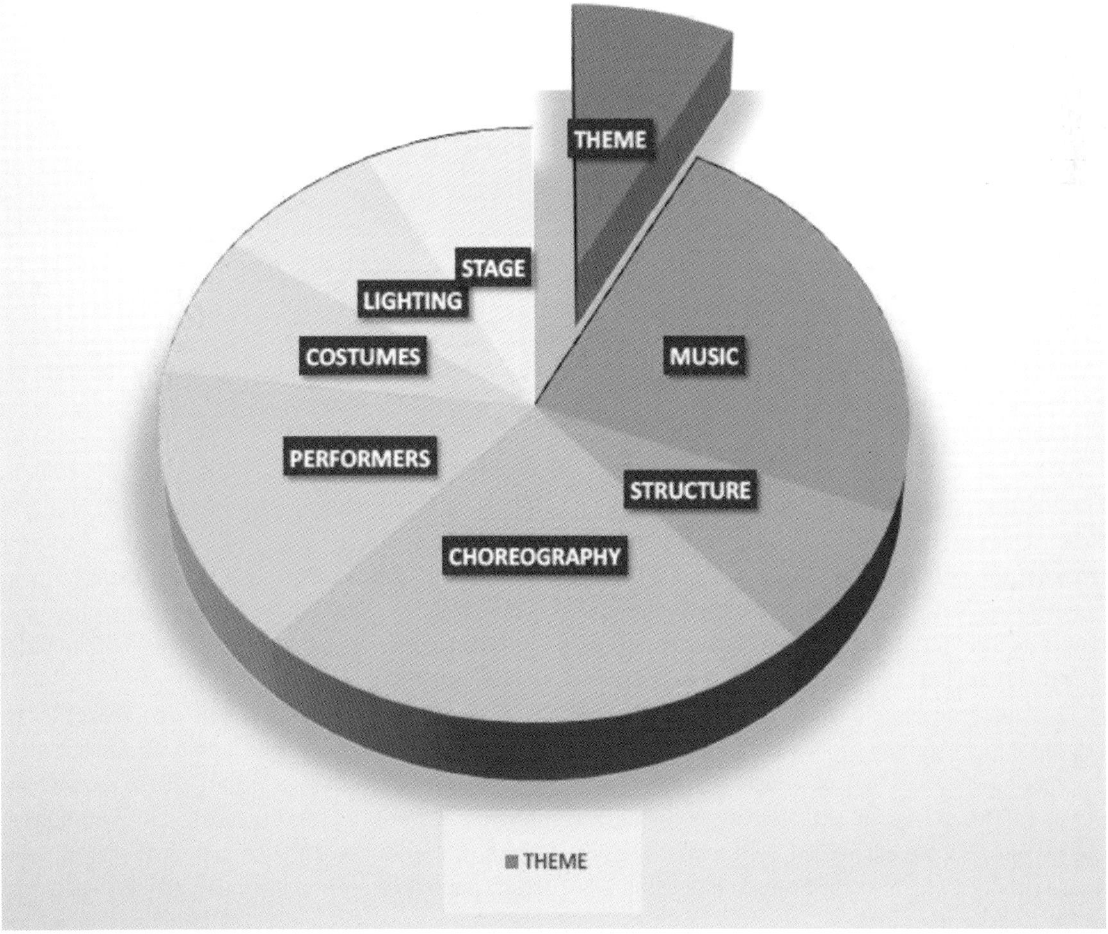

The 'theme' slice of the creative cake.

BOP company performing *Footprints in Jazz* at Emma Cons Hall, London (2014). BAFANA SOLOMAN MATEA

can need over a week's rehearsal time. Consequently, your theme also needs to reflect your time available to rehearse.

Finding and Choosing the Correct Music

Having the correct music is at the top of the creative process list. The music is a springboard to ignite all your initial visual pictures that can formulate through your rehearsals. In jazz dance the music is fundamental to your dance expression. As you have developed your listening skills, you will be able to identify more easily the content of the music. The beat will obviously set the pulse, but as jazz artists we are versed in syncopation, so our movements are influenced by the beat but not rigidly adhered to it. Identify the instruments that are at the front of the music – this could be the voice or an instrumental solo. These melodies need to be reflected in your choreography, maybe through an individual dancer or a tight ensemble section. The layers and textures will give you an emotional depth to your work; this could be lyrical and smooth or quick and staccato. Be aware of the highs and lows of the music or the sudden accents or musical pauses; these sounds are ideal to help your creative 'light' and 'shade'. It is often the contrast in the music that enables the most dramatic choreography.

Finally, do not be afraid to edit your music. There are many easy music editing programs available that can make the process of music editing reasonably straightforward. If possible, work with a composer or music producer. To work with a composer who can shape and develop the music as you create and develop your choreography is the dream ticket for all jazz dance creators.

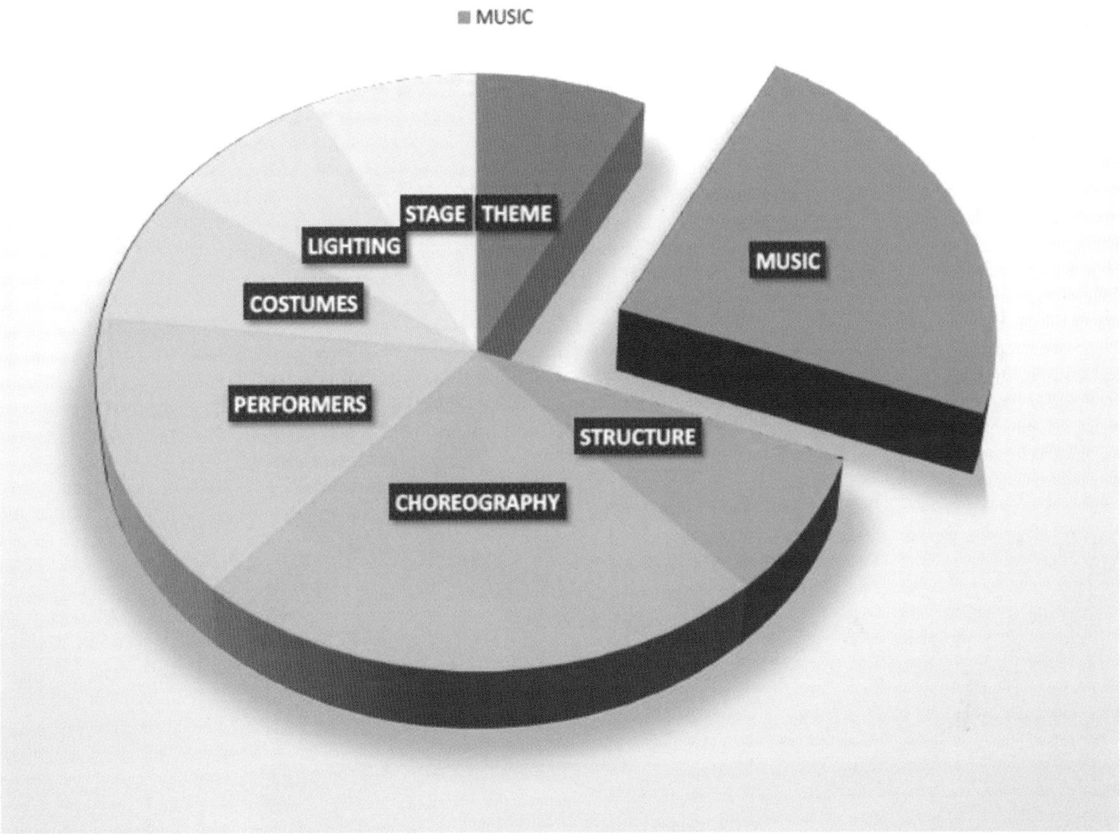

The 'music' slice.

Dollie Henry and Paul Jenkins performing the Spanish influenced duet *Aranjuez* from BOP Jazz Theatre *Touches of Miles*. BAFANA SOLOMAN MATEA

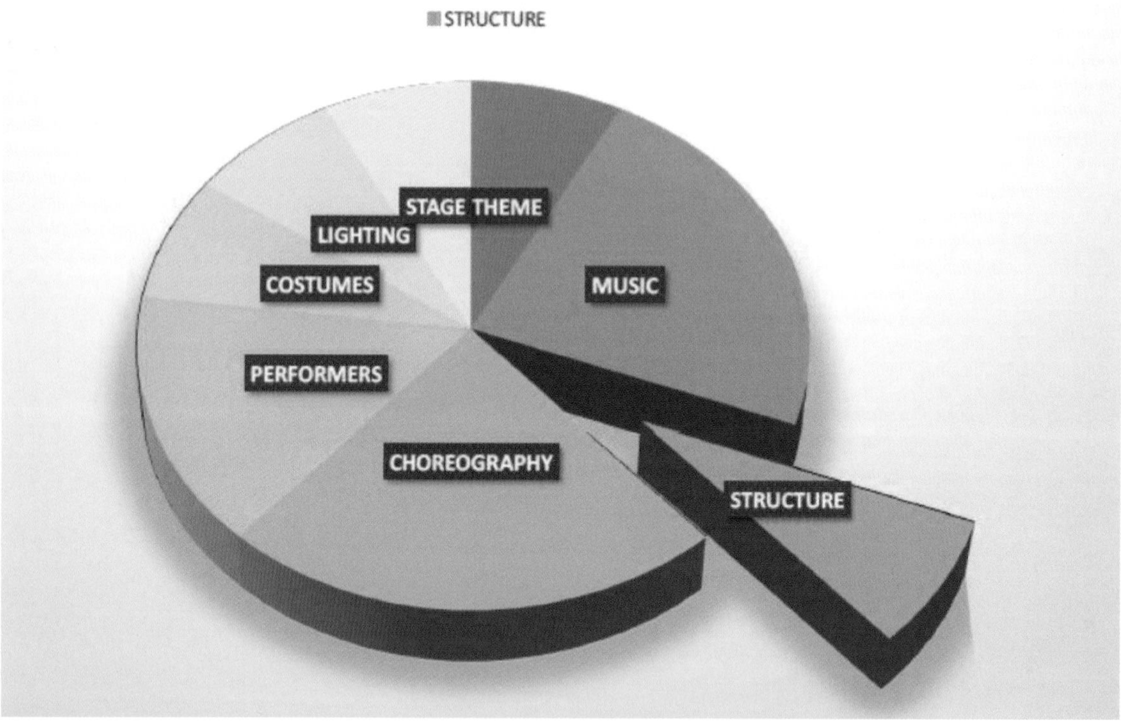

The 'structure' slice.

Matevz Cesen and Sarah Dos Santos performing BOP Theatre's narrative jazz dance pas de deux *A Woman's Blues*. SCOTT JORDANE

Defining and Structuring Your Dance Work

Defining your work is an important part of your pre-production, as this will assist you in developing a creative structure. For example, a piece of concert dance with no underlying narrative will need a structure totally dependent on the music; whereas for jazz theatre, the narrative is an essential part of your work, so often the structure is driven by both the music and the particular story line. For the former, your structure will follow the flow of the music; there generally is a beginning, a middle and an end, so this could easily form the basis of your structure. For the latter, your structure might be considered as theatrical scenes. The first scene could be introducing your dance characters or setting the theatrical location of your dance narrative. Structure is very important as it gives you an overview of the highs and lows or tension and release of your work. Remember, our job as dance creators is to keep our audiences engaged and connected to the show.

Choreographic Motifs and Themes of Movement

With all our dance creations, our choreography will develop over time as we improve through experience. When starting out as a choreographer it is

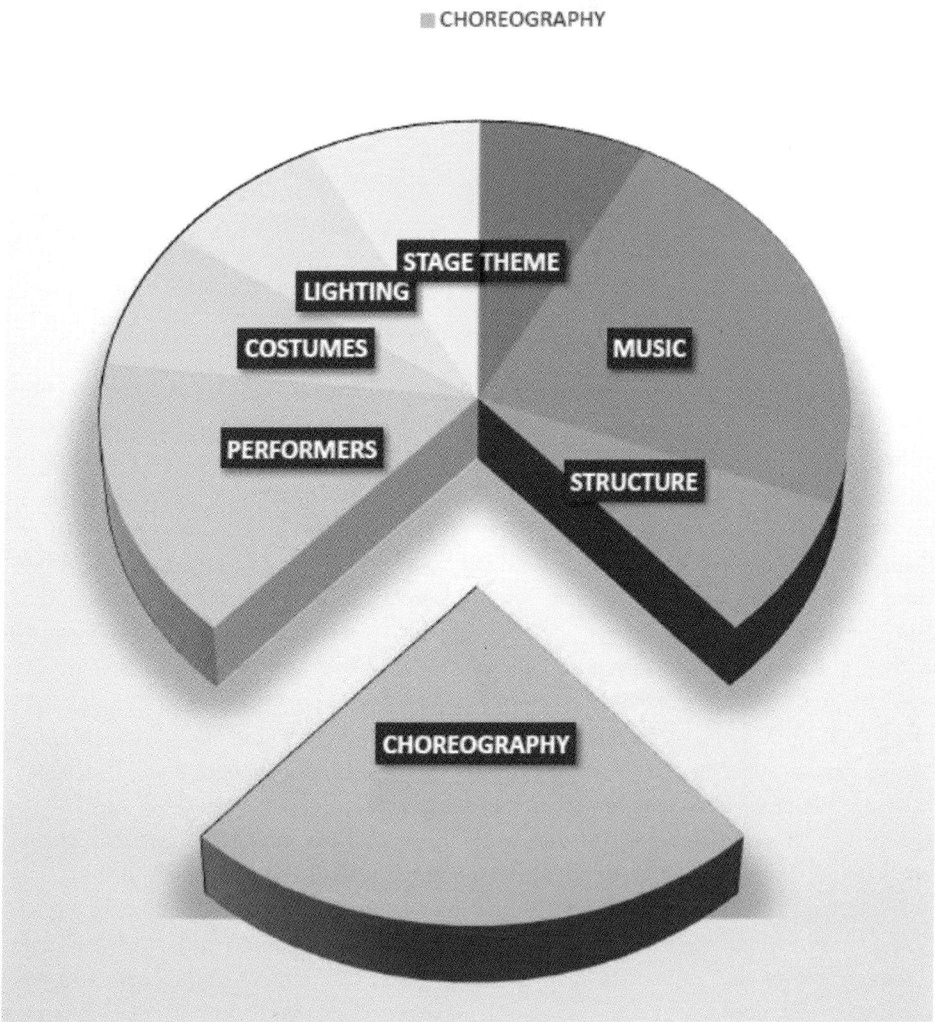

The 'choreography' slice.

Dancer performing the lyrical jazz piece *All Blues* from *Touches of Miles*. BRIAN APPIAH OBENG

essential that you have at least a few basic ideas of steps or movement that you bring to the first rehearsal. The first step or dance movement is often the most perplexing, so if you have previously visualized (when listening to the music) a few initial ideas, these will give you a springboard to leap from. Consider movements that you have used before and start to string these together. If you have developed a few dance motifs, work through these with your dancers and then start to insert them into your developing work. Once your initial creative ideas are expressed, then it is time to reflect and refine.

If your structured sections are for a solo dancer or the full dance ensemble, you can work these sections independently and bring them together at a later rehearsal. I cannot emphasize the importance of reviewing your work. Once your dance rehearsal is over your work does not stop there. You need to review and re-work, as necessary. Initially, in your mind's eye, imagine the next stage and then it is easier to develop in the rehearsal situation. Do not be afraid to cut those sections that clearly are not working. Nothing is lost – your creative dance motifs and choreography may well be used in a later section or indeed in another work. Finally, leave a space for, as Quincy Jones puts it, 'God to enter the room'. We are improvising artistes and, therefore, much of the work is developed through rehearsals. If your choreographic ideas are rigidly set, then the unexpected original idea that magically appears will simply not happen.

How Many Dancers Will the Creative Work Require?

The number of dancers you place in your work will have an impact on the piece and its outcome. Sometimes this is not easy if you're a dance teacher with fifty students that all need to be in the dance

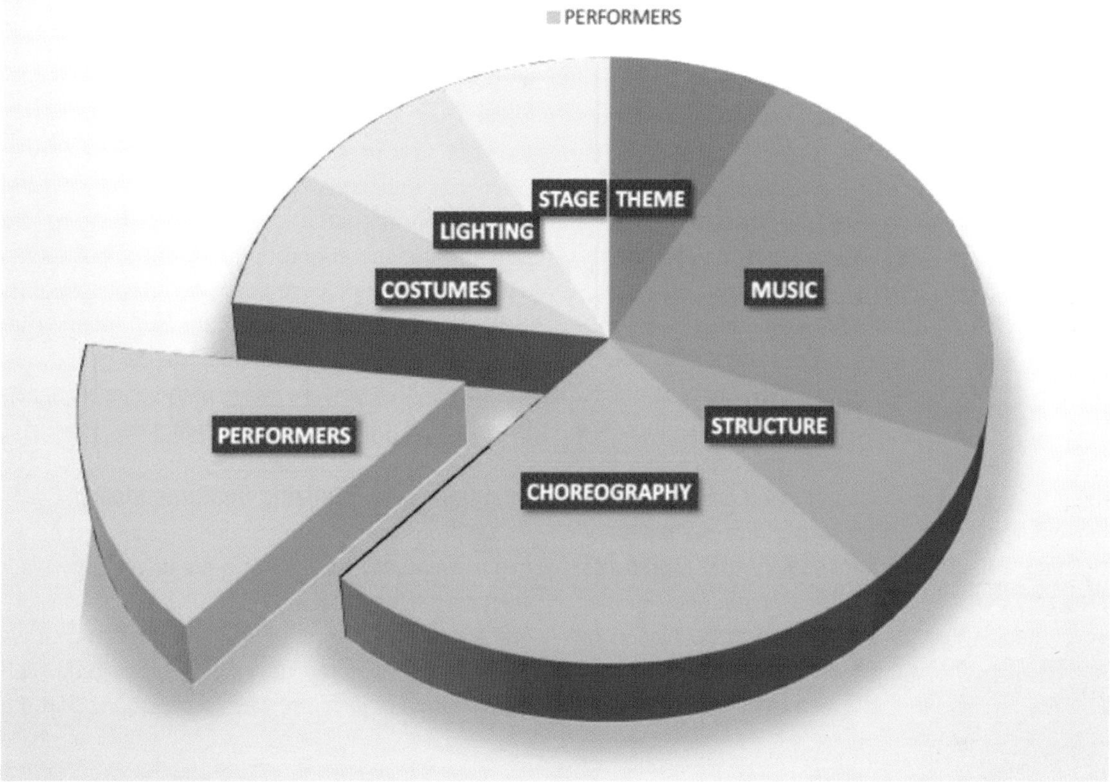

ABOVE: **The 'performers' slice.**

BELOW: **BOP dancers performing *Juba Jump*. African dance movement forms the main expression of the choreography.** BRENDON HANSFORD

number. However, using patterns and motifs appropriately and creating dance that allows for a journey of the dance narrative is where the clever creating and formations can come into play. For a large group, it is sensible to have smaller ensembles worked out. Staging becomes a very important part when working with a large group – be sure to use the whole of the performance area. Try not to make your choreography too 'flat', always use the depth of the stage. Consider how you get your ensembles and dancers on and off the performance area; if possible, do not always use the same entrance and exit points. With the more artistic narrative works, then the input of your dancers is essential. Characters may need to be developed, so you need dance performers who have the ability to perform in 'character' or bring a depth and connectivity that represents, and can transcend, emotions of real life. Further, your imagined dance ideas need to be placed on dancers who have the technical and performance abilities to execute them. Work with your dancers' techniques and abilities, not against them. In many ways choreography is a collaboration between you and the dancers, so do not be afraid to accept their ideas and suggestions, it might just be the 'golden moment' of your final creation. Finally, always try to work with dancers who share your creative vision and who are prepared to do the necessary work to execute your choreography as you imagined it. Keep a positive and creative atmosphere as you rehearse, support your dancers, encourage and affirm. That does not mean you cannot criticize them if they are wrong, just that you are aware of the creative sensitivity that surrounds all good rehearsals.

Designing and Realizing Costume Ideas

As we progress through our dance journey, then we might eventually be part of a creative team where we have the luxury of working with costume designers. However, when starting out it is often that we become the costume designer and costume realizer. That said, in many ways the designing of the

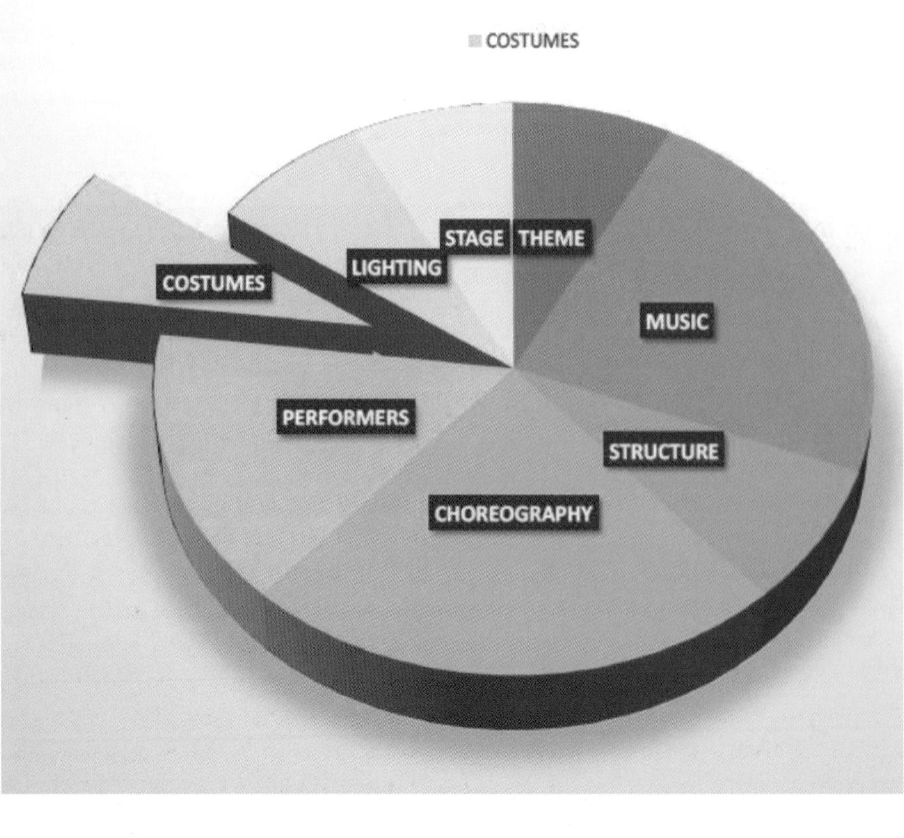

The 'costumes' slice.

Illaria Bellini performing in BOP Jazz Theatre repertoire *Daughters of Eve*. BAFANA SOLOMAN MATEA

costumes is fairly straightforward. Obviously, the music plays an important role here. For example, if your work is very much driven by the tapestry of an African theme, then the costumes could reflect this. If your piece is more directed to a lyrical composition and moves gently, once again the costumes can be created to further define and evoke a feeling of movement and flow, giving an added effect to the dance narrative.

If you have a story-driven narrative, then the setting and place of your work often drives the costume design. For example, if you have set your work in the 1920s, then flapper dresses or men's tails would be appropriate. Obviously, if you are lucky enough to have a costume designer/realizer on your team, they will be fully conversant with making costumes fit for the dancer to feel good and look good. Like the dance, the creating of costume can change as you develop the piece, but it is always good to have a starting point to work from.

Lighting Your Work

Often, as a dance creative we forget how important lighting can be in performance. It is generally left until we are in the performance space, where our time with the lighting operator is very limited. Therefore, plan your lighting ideas, write them down and forward your ideas to the lighting designer before your 'get in' to the dance theatre space. Most designers would have hung lights before your rehearsal, so if they are aware of your lighting intentions, then they can plan for this in pre-production. Lights can often set the mood for your dance, so choose your colours carefully. Transitions of light can also add atmosphere, as can big explosions of colour. Lighting designers can also cleverly mask areas of the stage, so for solos or smaller ensembles the stage can be a more intimate, defined area. Always time your lighting changes with the music. No point in having a blackout when the music reaches an abrupt halt if the stage has been plunged into

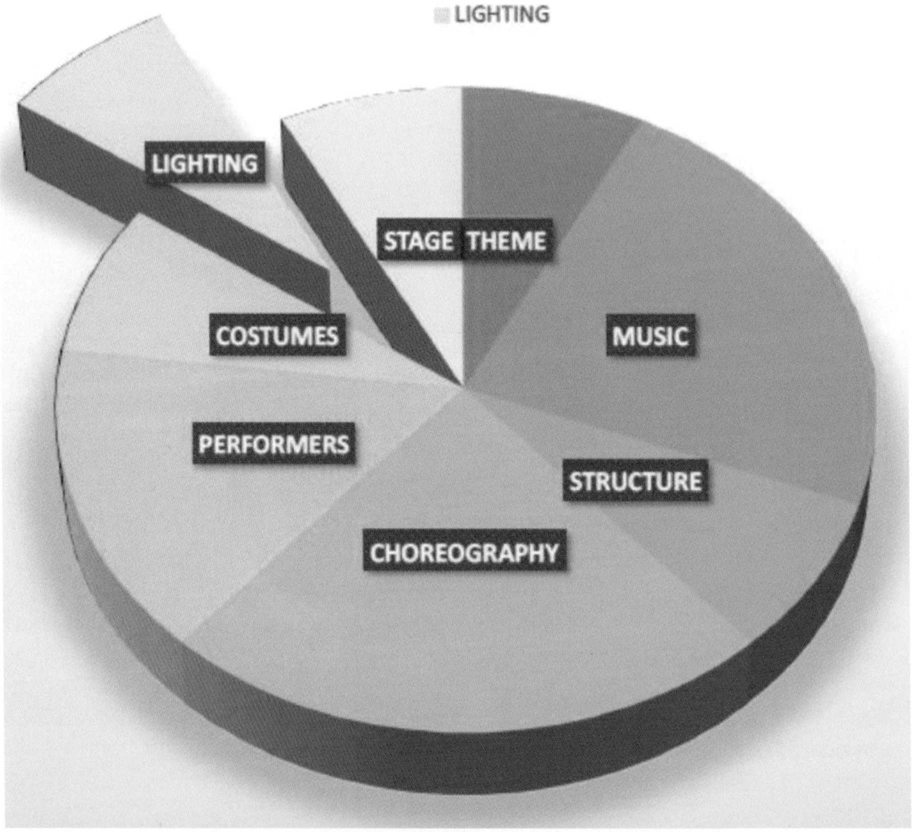

The 'lighting' slice.

BELOW: **Kimberlee Collicutt and Andrew Denton performing from *Directions.***
BRENDON HANSFORD

total darkness two seconds previously. In this day of developing technology, lights can do many amazing things. Most spaces will have a selection of lights and at least a few 'movers'; these are great not only for lighting effects, but also rapid changes of colour and beautiful transitions.

Set Design and Staging

More often than not, our early performance opportunities are programmed in dance spaces that have an open performance area. Obviously, in those productions there will be no need for a stage design.

If you are lucky to have a stage and the opportunity for a set, then planning is vital for success. If possible, work with a stage designer as they will have the technical know-how. Always be conscious that your set needs to be fit for dance and dancing. If you have a set that moves, this must be planned into your rehearsal schedule to prepare all your performers. Remember, under-stage light visibility is not always perfect, so you need to be able to move around the stage safely.

Props can also enhance your production. These are very much dependent on your particular dance narrative and can range from a simple flower to twenty chairs and four tables for a jazz club scene. As always, you need to plan how to move your dancers around these. If props need to be brought on to the stage as the performance progresses, make this part of your choreography, they can add a great visual element to your work.

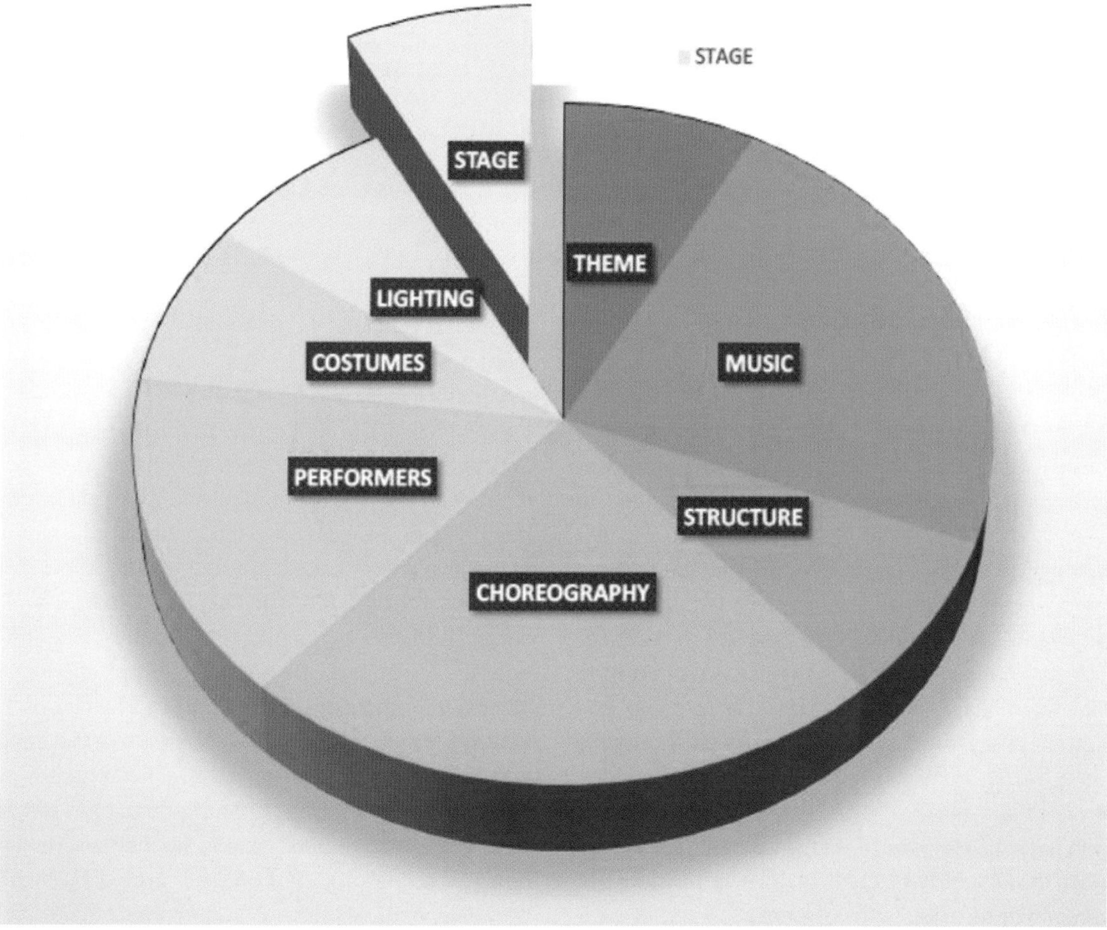

The 'stage' slice.

The character-driven jazz repertoire *Night in Tunisia* from BOP Jazz Theatre production *Dizzy Heights* (1999).

A MOMENT TO REVIEW AND RE-EVALUATE

As this book is reaching out to the dance student, professional dancer, dance teacher/practitioner and the jazz dance enthusiast, there is a need to review and re-evaluate the development and the long, complex journey of the jazz vernacular. As a practical guide, the aim of this book is to articulate an overview that is insightful, practical and educational. What is very clear, is that jazz is an art form like no other. Ultimately, jazz is an organic and improvisatory art form that requires us to engage on a higher creative and practical level. The inclusivity of jazz means that it is open to interpretation and delivery. However, if we are to relish and experience the jazz vernacular for all it is, it is imperative to remember its true source of innovation and inspiration. To lose the footing of the jazz expression and its unique aesthetic would be to negate the fundamental techniques and skills, improvisational flair, innate musicality and timing, and more importantly the distinctiveness that create that unique vibration and expression of jazz dance. As long as we can respect and honour the origins and the traditions of jazz, then the form will continue to be at the forefront of creative and artistic dance and theatre-making.

Jazz is a celebration of and explanation of cultural, social, political and economic identity – the lineage, the transitions, the styles, the form, the innovators, the practitioners, the black and white of it. Lest we forget, it is upon the shoulders of the early jazz pioneers and their natural creative impulse of expression and innovation, that the branches of the jazz art form have been able to flourish and today continue to be practised and performed by many dancers, and reinvented and shaped by many dance teachers and choreographers.

Samantha Tan taking flight in a stylized jazz jump. SIMON RICHARDSON

The gentlemen of Adam Parson Commonality Dance Company LA. In dance flow, sharing a motif of movement.

ADAM PARSON

It is fair to say that, due to cultural bias and appropriation, the black originators and important practitioners of jazz and tap dance have not always been given their due respect or, indeed, considered part of the creative lineage of jazz dance. The hope is that this practical guide clears those muddy waters somewhat, enabling us to investigate and elaborate all the jazz geniuses over the last two centuries.

Minstrelsy to MTV clearly exemplify the great diversity evident throughout the history of jazz. Authentic, social, modern, musical theatre, concert dance, jazz theatre and jazz fusion all belong under the same jazz umbrella, each branch developing a unique style that is reflected through individual expression and interpretation. A desire that all jazz artists aspire to attain and maintain, to continue developing a pathway and creative identity through the jazz dance expression.

One of the many benefits of writing this book on jazz dance and its inherent music is the opportunity to refine what is already known and yet reveal that which is unknown, accessing something new to draw from and be inspired by. As the saying goes, you never stop learning. Therefore, at the very least this book will offer a springboard for dancers and dance teachers alike, to further their own personal discovery and investigation of the dance, the music, the history and lineage, the innovators past and present and, more importantly, the expression and creative language of jazz evident in so much of dance today, making it possible to relish and enjoy, on so many levels, the fruits of the jazz tree.

Samantha Tan striking a stylized jazz pose. SIMON RICHARDSON

APPENDIX

FURTHER READING AND RESOURCES

READING BETWEEN THE LINES

There are many books and much information that offer viewpoints, opinions and insights, from differing experiences, cultural and social journeys and study material.

For an academic study, there are many streams that offer in-depth literature on the history of jazz from the 1800s onwards. If you have the time, it is worth searching and collating for your own references and knowledge. Increasing your knowledge and understanding of the dance, music and theatre of the jazz art form can further assist and inspire your own journey as a jazz dancer, teacher or choreographer.

As a starting point, here is a short list of material to enjoy and be inspired by.

Jazz Dance History

Jazz Dance – A History of the Roots and Branches by Lindsay Guarino and Wendy Oliver (2014)

Jazz Dance: The Story of American Vernacular by Marshall Stearns and Jean Stearns

The Swing Era: The Development of Jazz, 1930–45 by Gunther Schuller (history of jazz)

OPPOSITE: **Matevz Cesen performing a contemporary jazz dance *Directions* from BOP Jazz Theatre production *Miles Ahead*.** BRIAN APPIAH OBENG

Out of Africa in the Dance Has Many Faces by Walter Sorell (New York: Columbia Press)

Black Dance: From 1619 to Today by Lynne Fauley Emery (Princeton Book Company)

The History of Jazz by Ted Gioia (music)

Tap Roots: The Early History of Tap Dancing by Mark Knowles

Tap Dancing America: A Cultural History by Constance Valis Hill

What the Eye Hears: A History of Tap Dancing by Brian Seibert (Farrar, Straus and Giroux)

Tap Roots: The Early History of Tap Dancing by Mark Knowles (Jefferson, North Carolina: McFarland and Company Inc., 2002)

Steppin' on the Blues: The Visible Rhythms of African American Dance by Jacqui Malone (Urbana and Chicago: University of Illinois Press, 1996)

Marian Hannah Winter, 'Juba and American Minstrelsy' *Chronicles of the American Dance*, Paul Magriel, ed. (New York: Henry Holt and Company, 1948)

Dances That Describe Themselves by Susan Leigh Foster (University Press of New England)

I Want to be Ready: Improvised Dance as a Practice of Freedom by Danielle Goldman (University of Michigan Press)

Dancing Many Drums: Excavations in African American Dance by Thomas F. DeFrantz (University of Wisconsin Press)

Teaching Jazz Dance

Anthology of American Jazz Dance by Gus Giordano

Beginning Jazz Dance by James W. Robey

Frank Hatchett's Jazz Dance by Frank Hatchett, Nancy Myers Gitlin

Luigi's Jazz Warm Up: An Introduction to Jazz Style and Technique by Luigi Falco

Matt Mattox Book of Jazz Dance by Matt Mattox and Elizabeth Frich

Autobiographies: Jazz Dancers and Choreographers

Revelations: The Autobiography by Alvin Ailey

Alvin Ailey: A Life in Dance by Jennifer Dunning

Katherine Dunham: Dancing a Life by Joyce Aschenbrenner

Katherine Dunham: Pioneer of Black Dance by Barbara O'Connor

The Dance Claimed Me by Pearl Primus

Frankie Manning: Ambassador of Lindy Hop by Frankie Manning and Cynthia R. Millman

Class Act: The Jazz Life of Cholly Atkins by Cholly Atkins and Jacqui Malone

Swinging at The Savoy – The Memoir of a Jazz Dancer by Norma Miller

Steps in Time: An Autobiography – Fred Astaire by Fred Astaire

The Astaires: Fred and Adele by Kathleen Riley

Sammy: The Autobiography of Sammy Davis, Jr by Sammy Davis Jr, Burt and Jane Boyar

In Black and White: The Life of Sammy Davis by Wil Haygood

Unsung Genius: The Passion of a Dancer-Choreographer Jack Cole by Glenn Loney

Dance with Demons: The Life of Jerome Robbins by Greg Lawrence

Jerome Robbins: His Life, His Theater, His Dance by Deborah Jowitt

Jerome Robbins: That Broadway Man by Christine Conrad

All His Jazz: The Life and Death Of Bob Fosse by Martin Gottfried

Razzle Dazzle: The Life and Work of Bob Fosse by Kevin Boyd Grubb

The Josephine Baker Story by Ean Wood

Josephine by Josephine Baker, Jo Bouillon and Marina Fitzpatrick

Gene Kelly: A Biography by Clive Hirschhorn

Gene Kelly: A Life of Dance and Dreams by Alvin Yudoff

Gregory Hines: Entertainer (Black Americans of Achievement) by Dennis Abrams

Brotherhood in Rhythm: The Jazz Tap Dancing of the Nicholas Brothers by Constance Valis Hill

Mr Bojangles: The Biography of Bill Robinson by Jim Haskins

Savion: My Life in Tap by Savion Glover and Bruce Weber

TAP! The Greatest Tap Dance Stars and Their Stories 1900–55 by Rusty Frank

Autobiographies: Jazz Musicians, Composers and Singers

Miles: The Autobiography of Miles Davis by Miles Davis and Quincy Troupe

Pops: The Life of Louis Armstrong by Terry Teachout

Music is My Life: Louis Armstrong, Autobiography, and American Jazz by Daniel Stein

Duke Ellington: A Spiritual Biography (Lives and Legacies) by Janna Tull Steed

Music is my Mistress (Autobiography of Duke Ellington) by Edward Kennedy Ellington

Billie Holiday: A Biography by Meg Greene

Lady Sings the Blues – Billie Holiday by David Ritz

Ella Fitzgerald: A Biography of the First Lady of Jazz by Stuart Nicholson

Stormy Weather: The Life of Lena Horne by James Garth

Frank Sinatra: The Man, the Music, the Legend by Jeanne Fuchs and Ruth Prigozy

Q – The Autobiography of Quincy Jones by Quincy Jones

Dizzy: Autobiography of Dizzy Gillespie by Dizzy Gillespie and Alfred Fraser

To Be, or Not ... to Bop by Dizzy Gillespie and Al Fraser

Paul Bailey, Penny Ashcroft and David Olton performing the character-driven BOP Jazz Theatre production to the music of Dizzy Gillespie *Dizzy Heights* (1998).

FILMS AND DOCUMENTARIES WITH A JAZZ TWIST

Jazz Dance Films, Musicals and Documentaries

All that Jazz (1979)
Director: Bob Fosse. Producers: Columbia Pictures/Twentieth Century Fox

An American in Paris (1951)
Director: Vincente Minnelli. Producers: MGM

A Chorus Line (1985)
Director: Richard Attenborough. Producers: Embassy Pictures/Polygram Pictures

Anchors Aweigh (1945)
Director: George Sidney. Producers: MGM

Bojangles (2001)
Director: Joseph Sargent. Producers: MGM Television/Darric Productions

Born to Dance (1936)
Director: Roy Del Ruth. Producers: MGM

The Broadway Melody (1929)
Director: Harry Beaumont. Producers: MGM

Cab Calloway's Hi-De-Ho (1934)
Director: Fed Walker. Producers: Paramount Pictures

Cabaret (1972)
Director: Bob Fosse. Producers: Allied Artists Pictures/ABC Pictures

Carmen Jones (1954)
Director: Otto Preminger. Producers: Otto Preminger Films

Chicago (2002)
Director: Rob Marshall. Producers: Miramax/Producers Circle

Dancing Lady (1933)
Director: Robert Leonard. Producers: MGM

Dreamgirls (2006)
Director: Bill Condon. Producers: DreamWorks/Paramount Pictures

The Cotton Club (1984)
Director: Francis Ford Coppola. Producers: Zoetrope Studios/PSO

42nd Street (1933)
Director: Lloyd Bacon. Producers: Warner Bros

The Greatest Showman (2017)
Director: Michael Gracey. Producers: Chernin Entertainment Twentieth Century Fox

Guys and Dolls (1955)
Director: Joseph Mankiewicz. Producers: Samuel Goldwyn Company

Idlewild (2006)
Director: Bryan Barber. Producers: Atlas Entertainment/HBO Films

La La Land (2006)
Director: Damien Chazelle. Producers: Summit Entertainment

Lady Sings the Blues (1972)
Director: Sidney J Furie. Producers: Jobete Productions/Motown Productions/Paramount Pictures

Mo Better Blues (1990)
Director: Spike Lee. Producers: 40 Acres and a Mule/Universal Pictures

Moulin Rouge (2001)
Director: Buz Luhrmann. Producers: Twentieth Century Fox/Bazmark Films

New York New York (1977)
Director: Martin Scorsese. Producers: Chartoff-Winkler Productions

On the Town (1949)
Director: Gene Kelly/Stanley Donen. Producers: MGM

Porgy and Bess (1959)
Director: Otto Preminger. Producers: Samuel Goldwyn Company

A Rage in Harlem (1991)
Director: Bill Duke. Producers: Miramax/Palace Pictures

Round Midnight (1986)
Director: Bertrand Tavernier. Producers: Little Bear/PECF

Shall we Dance (2004)
Director: Peter Chelsom. Producers: Miramax

Silk Stocking (1957)
Director: Rouben Mamoulian. Producers: MGM

Singing in the Rain (1952)
Director: Gene Kelly/Stanley Donen. Producers: MGM

Stormy Weather (1943)
Director: Andrew I. Stone. Producers: Twentieth Century Fox

Sweet Charity (1969)
Director: Bob Fosse. Producers: Universal Pictures

Swing Time (1936)
Director: George Stevens. Producers: RKO Radio Pictures

Tap – with Gregory Hines (1989)
Director: Nick castle. Producers: Beco Films/TriStar Pictures

That's Dancing! (1985)
Director: Jack Haley Jr. Producers: MGM

The Nicholas Brothers – We Sing We Dance (1992)
Director: Chris Bould/Michael Martin. Producers: Independent Film Picture Music International

Thoroughly Modern Millie! (1967)
Director: George Roy Hill. Producers: Universal Pictures/Ross Hunter Productions

Top Hat (1935)
Director: Mark Sandrich. Producers: RKO Radio Pictures

West Side Story (1961)
Director: Jerome Robbins/Robert Wise. Producers: The Mirisch Corporation/Seven Arts Productions

White Nights (1985)
Director: Taylor Hackford. Producers: Columbia Pictures

The Wiz (1978)
Director: Sidney Lumet. Producers: Universal Pictures/Motown Pictures

Ziegfeld Follies (1945)
Director: Lemuel Ayers/Roydel Ruth. Producers: MGM

Jazz Music Films and Documentaries

Anita O'Day: The Life of a Jazz Singer (2007)
A documentary film by Ian McCrudden. Producers: Robbie Cavonlia/Melissa Davis

The Coltrane Legacy (1987)
A documentary film. Directed by David Chertok

Art Pepper: Notes on a Jazz Survivor (1982)
A documentary film. Directed by Don McGlynn

Chasing Trane (2016)
A documentary film. Directed by John Scheinfeld

Charles Mingus: Triumph of the Underdog (1998)
A documentary film. Directed by Don McGlynn

Dexter Gordon – More Than You Know Underdog (1996)
A documentary film. Directed by Don McGlynn

Duke Ellington; Reminiscing in Tempo (1992)
A documentary film. Directed by Robert Levi

Duke Ellington and his Famous Orchestra; A Drum is a Woman (1962)
BBC documentary film

Ella Fitzgerald: Something to Live For (1999)
A documentary film. Directed by Charlotte Zwern

I Called him Morgan (2016)
A documentary film. Directed by Kasper Collin

Jazz on a Summer's Day (2016)
A documentary film. Directed by Bert Stern and Aram Avakian

Jazz (2001)
A documentary TV series. Directed by Ken Burns

Jazz: The Intimate Art (1977)
A documentary film. Directed by Robert Drew

Let's get Lost – Biography of Chet Baker (1998)
A documentary film. Directed by Bruce Weber

The Miles Davis Story (2001)
A Channel 4 documentary film. Directed by Mike Dibb

Nat King Cole – Afraid of the Dark (2014)
A documentary film. Directed by Jon Brewer

On the Road with Duke Ellington (1974)
A documentary film. Directed by Robert Drew

Quincy – Biography of Quincy Jones (2018)
A documentary film. Directed by Alan Hicks and Rashida Jones

Saint John Coltrane (2004)
A documentary film. Directed by Lol Lovett

Sidney Bechet: Treat it Gentle (2007)
A documentary film. Directed by Alan Lewens

Stan Kenton: Artistry in Rhythm (2011)
A documentary film. Directed by Graham Carter

Thelonious Monk; Straight no Chaser (1998)
A documentary film. Directed by Charlotte Zwerin

The Long Night of Lady Day – Biography of Billie Holiday (1984)
A documentary film. Directed by John Jeremy

The Year That Changed Jazz (2009)
A documentary film. Directed by Paul Bernays

A SHORTLIST OF WORTHY JAZZ MUSIC ARTISTS AND COMPOSERS

If you are not yet down with the rhythm and rhyme of jazz music, here is a list of jazz artists, musicians, bands and composers, whose names are worth checking out.

There are a multitude of jazz music categories to explore, from the African drum beat, New Orleans and ragtime, to swing, cool, bebop, experimental, jazz fusion to soul, funk and rnb all the way through to latest grooves created by the jazz music makers of our present generation.

One question most asked of me is, 'where do I find my jazz music to create and teach upon?' As a jazz choreographer, I am lucky enough to be married to, and co-create with, a jazz composer and jazz musician, so I struck lucky. It is true, we all have differing taste in music and my choice of music is maybe someone else's earache. For as long as I can remember, jazz music has surrounded me; from my childhood it was all around me in its various forms at home, in my headphones and underlines all my choreography today. For the last fifty years, jazz music has been my musical mentoring dance partner. That's not to say I'm not appreciative of all other musical forms. I listen to everything from classical music and most world music. All music has a personal story and message to share and inspire.

However, as many dancers and teachers who learn and teach jazz are not exposed to jazz music, be that in life or within the education of jazz dance, it can be a daunting process.

Where to Start to Find Your Aural Relationship With Jazz Music

First step (literally) is simply start by listening to jazz music, and I do not mean just popular chart music. As jazz dancers, teachers and choreographers, we owe it to the dance to understand that the tradition of jazz dance is founded in the music – that of jazz music. Jazz music paints colour into the dance we produce as jazz exponents.

Exposing your aural awareness and sensibilities to the wonder of jazz music provides yet another outlet for exploring and expanding your jazz dance creativity, connecting to the real inspiration of movement, that of the music. The soundscape of jazz music and its resonance readily provides the perfect canvas for inventive and original jazz dance creation. The more you dig the music of jazz, the more you will unfold in the movement and expression of jazz dance.

Paul Jenkins leading his Youth Jazz Orchestra in a live performance at St John Smith Concert Hall, London.

Traditional Jazz

Artist	*Instrument*	*Albums*
Armstrong, Louis	Trumpet	*The Hot Fives*
		Ella and Louis
		Louis Armstrong and Duke Ellington
Bechet, Sidney	Clarinet/Composer	*Texas Moaner Blues*
		Muskrat Ramble
Beiderbecke, Bix	Trumpet	*Bix Beiderbecke 1924–30*
		Bix and Tram
Dodds, Johnny	Clarinet, saxophone	*Clarinet Wobble*
Hines, Earl	Piano	*Louis Armstrong and Earl Hines*
		Swingin' Down
Johnson, James P	Piano	*James P. Johnson 1921–26*
Joplin, Scott	Piano	*Maple Leaf Rag*
		The Ragtime Dance
Keppard, Freddie	Cornet	
Manone, Wingy	Trumpet	*The Wingy Manone Collection*
Miley, Bubber	Trumpet	*Black and Tan Fantasy*
		Creole Love Call
Morton, Jelly Roll	Piano/Vocals	*Jelly Roll Morton 1930–39*
		Kansas City Stomp
Oliver, Joe 'King'	Cornet	*King Oliver Vol. 1 1923–29*
		King Oliver and his Orchestra
Ory, Kid	Trombone/Vocals	*Kid Ory's Creole Jazz Band*
		The Legendary Kid
Singleton, Zutty	Drummer	*Stormy Weather*
Smith, Willie 'The Lion'	Piano/Vocals	*The Lion's in Town*
		Pork and Beans
Spanier, Muggsy	Cornet	*The Great Sixteen*
Teagarden, Jack	Trombone/Vocals	*I Gotta' Right to Sing the Blues*
Trumbauer, Frankie	Saxophone	*For no Reason at All*
		Georgia on My Mind
Waller, Fats	Piano/Vocal	*The Joint is Jumpin'*
		The Definitive Fats Waller

Swing Jazz

Artist	*Instrument*	*Albums*
Eldridge, Roy	Trumpet	*After You've Gone*
		Roy and Diz
Ellington, Duke	Band Leader/Piano	*Black, Brown and Beige*
		A Drum is a Women
		The Far East Suite
		Sacred Concerts
		New Orleans Suite

Goodman, Benny	Clarinet	*The Birth of Swing*
		Live at Carnegie Hall
Hampton, Lionel	Bandleader/Vibraphone	*Lionel Hampton 1939–40*
		Hamp in Harlem
Hawkins, Coleman	Saxophone	*Coleman Hawkins encounters Ben Webster*
		The Hawk in Europe
Hefti, Neal	Arranger/Trumpet	*Hefti in Gotham City*
		Basie
Hines, Earl	Piano	*Earl Hines Piano Solos 1928–40*
		Earl Hines Plays Duke Ellington
Hodges, Johnny	Saxophone	*Ellingtonia '56*
		Everybody knows Johnny Hodges
James, Harry	Trumpet/Bandleader	*Young Man with a Horn*
		Harry's Choice
McShann, Jay	Piano	*Kansas City Memories*
Sims, Zoot	Saxophone	*The Brothers*
		Locking Horns
Tatum, Art	Piano	*The Genius of Art Tatum*
		Piano Starts Here
Terry, Clark	Trumpet	*Serenade to a Bus Seat*
		Memories of Duke
Tizol, Juan	Trombone	*Journey into Love*
		Caravan
Williams, Cootie	Trumpet	*Cootie Williams and his Orchestra 1941–44*
Wilson, Teddy	Piano	*Pre and Teddy*
		Teddy Wilson featuring Billie Holiday
Young, Lester	Saxophone	*Pres and Teddy*

Bebop

Artist	*Instrument*	*Albums*
Brown, Clifford	Trumpet	*The Beginning and the End*
		Clifford Brown with Strings
Chambers, Paul	Bass	*Chambers Music*
		Bass on Top
Christian, Charlie	Guitar	*The Genius of Charlie Christian*
Cobb, Jimmy	Drums	*Sophisticated Swing*
Dorham, Kenny	Trumpet	*Kenny Dorham Quintet*
		Afro-Cuban
Getz, Stan	Saxophone	*Grooving High*
		Diz and Getz
Gillespie, Dizzy	Trumpet	*Groovin' High*
		Birks Works
		Gillespiana
		Afro
Gordon, Dexter	Saxophone	*The Duel*

Bebop *(continued)*

Artist	*Instrument*	*Albums*
Jones, Philly Joe	Drums	*Drums Around the World*
		Drum Sons
Konitz, Lee	Saxophone	*Lee Konitz and Stan Getz*
		Lee Konitz with Strings
Monk, Thelonious	Piano	*Thelonious Monk Trio*
		Straight No Chaser
Moody, James	Saxophone	*Moody's Move for Love*
		Moody 48
Navarro, Fats	Trumpet	*Miles Davis/Dizzy Gillespie/*
		Fats Navarro – Trumpet Giants
Parker, Charlie	Saxophone	*The Charlie Parker story*
		Now's the Time
		Charlie Parker with Strings
Pass, Joe	Guitar	*Joy Spring*
		Portraits of Duke Ellington
Pepper, Art	Saxophone	*Art Pepper Meets the Rhythm Section*
Powell, Bud	Piano	*The Genius of Bud Powell*
Rodney, Red	Trumpet	*Bird Lives*
Rollins, Sonny	Saxophone	*Saxophone Colossus*
		Alternatives
Stitt, Sonny	Saxophone	*The Saxophones of Sonny Stitt*
		Sonny Stitt with the Oscar Peterson Trio

Big Band

Artist	*Instrument*	*Albums*
Basie, Count	Bandleader/Piano	*Count Basie at Newport*
		Atomic Mr Basie
Bellson, Louis	Bandleader/Drums	*The Louis Bellson Explosion*
		Jazz Giants
Calloway, Cab	Bandleader/Vocalist	*Cab Calloway 1932–34*
		Cab Calloway 1940–41
Dorsey, Tommy	Bandleader/Trombone	*Well, Git it*
		The Best of Tommy Dorsey
Ellington, Duke	Bandleader/Piano	*Black, Brown and Beige*
		A Drum is a Women
		The Far East Suite
		Sacred Concerts
		New Orleans Suite
Goodman, Benny	Bandleader/Clarinet	*The Birth of Swing*
		Live at Carnegie Hall
Hampton, Lionel	Bandleader/Vibraphone	*Lionel Hampton 1939–40*
		Hamp in Harlem

Henderson, Fletcher	Bandleader	*Louis Armstrong with Fletcher Henderson*
		Fletcher Henderson and the Dixie Stompers
Herman, Woody	Bandleader/Trumpet	*The Thundering Herds 1945–47*
		Woody's Winners
Thad Jones/Mel Lewis Orchestra	Bandleaders Trumpet/ Drums	*Live at the Village Vanguard*
		Live in Munich
Kenton, Stan	Bandleader/Piano	*Retrospective*
		Cuban Fire
Lunceford, Jimmie	Bandleader/Saxophone	*Rhythm is Our Business*
McConnell, Rob	Bandleader/Trombone	*The Boss Brass*
		Big Band Jazz
Miller, Glen	Bandleader/Trombone	*American Patrol*
		Moonlight Serenade
Rich, Buddy	Bandleader/Drums	*His Legendary 1947–48 Orchestra*
Webb, Chick	Bandleader/Drums	*Chick Webb a Legend Vol. 1*
Whiteman, Paul	Bandleader/Composer	*Whispering*
		Three O'Clock in the Morning

Mainstream Jazz

Artist	*Instrument*	*Albums*
Adderley, Julian (Cannonball)	Alto saxophone	*Somethin' Else*
		Cannonball and Coltrane
		At the Lighthouse
Baker, Chet	Trumpet	*My Funny Valentine*
		Someday my Prince will Come
Blakey, Art	Drums	*A Night in Tunisia*
		Album of the Year
		Oh, By the Way
Brown, Clifford	Trumpet	*The Beginning and the End*
		Clifford Brown with Strings
Brubeck, Dave	Piano	*Time Out*
		Mr Broadway
Coltrane, John	Tenor saxophone	*Blue Trane*
		My Favorite Things
		A Love Supreme
Davis, Miles	Trumpet	*Round about Midnight*
		Kinda Blue
		Porgy and Bess
		Sketches of Spain
		Tutu
Evans, Bill	Piano	*At the Village Vanguard*
		Bill Evans Trio with Symphony Orchestra
Hubbard, Freddie	Trumpet	*First Light*
		Super Blue

Mainstream Jazz *(continued)*

Artist	*Instrument*	*Albums*
Jarrett, Keith	Piano	*Expectations*
		Standards Vol. 1
Johnson, JJ	Trombone/Composer	*Four Trombones*
		Say When
Marsalis, Branford	Saxophone	*Crazy People Music*
Marsalis, Wynton	Trumpet	*Father Time*
		Resolution to Swing
		From Plantation to Penitentiary
Mingus, Charles	Double bass	*Thirteen Pictures*
		Big Band Charlie Mingus
Montgomery, Wes	Guitar	*Incredible Jazz Guitar*
		Fusion
Morgan, Lee	Trumpet	*The Sidewinder*
		Top Cat
Peterson, Oscar	Piano	*Plays Porgy and Bess*
		Nigerian Marketplace
Redman, Dewey	Saxophone	*Look for the Black Star*
		African Venus
Reinhardt, Django	Guitar	*Bruxelles*
		Swing Guitar
Roach, Max	Drums	*Brownie Speaks*
		To the Max
Shorter, Wayne	Saxophone	*High Life*
		Algeria

Contemporary Jazz

Artist	*Instrument*	*Albums*
Alexander, Monty	Piano	*Triple Treat*
		Caribbean Circle
Ayers, Roy	Drums	*Everybody Loves Sunshine*
		Step into Our Life
Beniot, David	Piano	*Every Step of the Way*
		Full Circle
Benson, George	Guitar/Vocals	*Breezin'*
		Big Boss Sound
Blood, Sweat and Tears	Ensemble	*Brand New Day*
		The Essential Blood, Sweat and Tears
Botti, Chris	Trumpet	*Chris Botti in Boston*
		Impressions
Brecker, Brothers –	Tenor saxophone	*Straphangin'*
Michael and Randy	Trumpet	*Out of the Loop*

Browne, Tom	Trumpet	*Browne Sugar*
		Love Approach
Camilo, Michel	Piano	*Why Not?*
		On the Other Hand
Grusin, Dave	Piano/Composer	*Homage to Duke*
		The Gershwin Connection
Hancock, Herbie	Piano	*Maiden Voyage*
		Head Hunters
		Gershwin's World
Hargrove, Roy	Trumpet	*Diamond in the Rough*
		Directions in Music Live at Massey Hall
Headhunters, The	Ensemble	*Headhunters*
		Survival of the Fittest
Incognito	Ensemble	*Positivity*
		Eleven
James, Bob	Keyboards/Composer	*Double Vision*
		Ivory Coast
Jones, Quincy	Composer/Trumpet	*The Dude*
		Q's Jook Joint
Jordan, Ronnie	Guitar	*The Antidote*
		The Quiet Revolution
Klugh, Earl	Guitar	*Dream Come True*
		Living Inside Your Love
Laws, Hurbert	Flute	*My Time Will Come*
Laws, Ronnie	Saxophone	*Flame*
		Natural Laws
Lewis, Ramsey	Pianist/Composer	*The In Crowd*
		Urban Nights
M Base Collective	Ensemble	*Anatomy of the Groove*
Metheny, Pat	Guitar	*Travels*
		The Road to You
Miller, Marcus	Bass guitar	*Silver Rain*
		Tutu
Pastorius, Jaco	Bass guitar	*Live in Italy*
		Honesty
Sample, Joe	Piano	*Invitation*
		The Pecan Tree
Sanborn, Dave	Saxophone	*Voyeur*
		Hearsay
Snarky Puppy	Ensemble	*We Like it Here*
		Family Dinner
Spyro Gyra	Ensemble	*Morning Dance*
		20/20
Standring, Chris	Guitar	*Electric Wonderland*
		Don't Talk, Dance

Contemporary Jazz *(continued)*

Artist	*Instrument*	*Albums*
Washington Jr, Grover	Saxophone	*Winelight*
		Time Out of Mind
Watts, Ernie	Saxophone	*Sanctuary*
		Alive
Weather Report	Ensemble	*Heavy Weather*
		Procession
Whalum, Kirk	Saxophone	*Joined at the Hip*
		Human Nature

Orchestrated, Symphonic and Film Jazz

Artist	*Instrument*	*Albums*
Blanchard, Terence	Trumpet/Composer	*The Malcolm X Jazz Suite*
		Requiem for Katrina
		Breathless
Ellington, Duke	Piano/Bandleader/ Composer	*Black, Brown and Beige Suite*
Evans, Gil	Arranger	*Sketches of Spain*
		There Comes a Time
Grusin, Dave	Piano/Composer	*The Nutcracker Suite*
Jones, Quincy	Trumpet/Bandleader/ Composer/Producer	*On Golden Pond*
		Tootsie
O'Farrill, Arturo	Piano /Composer	*Song for Chico*
		Three Revolutions
Ogerman, Claus	Composer	*Homage to Duke*
		Gershwin Connects
		West Side Story
		The Colour Purple
		The Wiz
		Roots
		The Italian Job
		City Scape
		Aranjuez
Russell, George	Composer	*Living Time*
		Timeline
		It's About Time
Schifrin, Lalo	Composer	*Jazz Suite*
		Gillespiana
		Metamorphosis

Jazz Vocalists

Artist	*Instrument*	*Albums*
Bridgewater, Dee Dee	Vocalist	*Afro Blue*
		Red Earth
Carter, Betty	Vocalist	*At the Village Vanguard*
		It's Not About the Melody
Cole, Nat King	Vocalist/Piano	*Lush Life*
		Big Band Cole
Connick Jr, Harry	Vocalist/Piano	*Blue Light, Red Light*
		Only You, in Concert
Downing, Will	Vocalist	*Moods*
		A Love Supreme
Eckstine, Billy	Band Leader/Vocals	*I Want to Talk About You*
		No Cover, No Minimum
Elias, Eliane	Vocalist/Piano	*Paulistana*
		Dance of Time
Fitzgerald, Ella	Vocalist	*The Complete Songbooks*
		The Best of Ella Fitzgerald
Holiday, Billie	Vocalist	*Billie Holiday, the Voice of Jazz*
		Lady Sings the Blues
Horne, Lena	Vocalist	*Stormy Weather*
		Porgy and Bess
Gardot, Melody	Vocalist	*My One and Only Thrill*
		The Absence
Jarreau, Al	Vocalist/Composer	*This Time*
		High Crime
		Tenderness
Jordan, Louis	Vocalist /Saxophone	*At the Swing Cats Ball*
		Five Guys Named Moe
Krall, Diana	Vocalist	*The Look of Love*
		From this Moment On
		Quiet Nights
		A Night in Paris
Laine, Cleo	Vocalist	*Woman Talk*
Lundy, Carmen	Vocalist	*Moment to Moment*
		Changes
Martin, Claire	Vocalist	*When Lights are Low*
		Too Much in Love to Care
McRae, Carmen	Vocalist	*Just a Little Lovin'*
		Carmen Sings Monk
O'Day, Anita	Vocalist	*Swings Cole Porter*
		Rules of the Road
Porter, Gregory	Vocalist	*Water*
		Liquid Spirit

Jazz Vocalists *(continued)*

Artist	*Instrument*	*Albums*
Reeves, Dianne	Vocalist	*The Calling*
		Beautiful Life
Simone, Nina	Vocalist/Piano	*Nina Simone in Concert*
		The Best of Nina Simone
Smith, Bessie	Vocalist	*Kitchen Man*
		The Undisputed Queen of The Blues
Spalding, Esperanza	Vocalist/Bass	*Radio Music City*
		Exposure
Tormé, Mel	Vocalist	*The Ellington and Basie Songbooks*
		Round Midnight
Vaughan, Sarah	Vocalist/Piano	*16 Most Requested Songs*
		Misty
		Duke Ellington Songbook
Washington, Dinah	Vocalist	*The Dinah Washington Story*
		Unforgettable
Wilson, Cassandra	Vocalist	*Dance to the Drums Again*
		Silver Pony
Wilson, Nancy	Vocalist	*Lush Life*
		But Beautiful

Dancer performing with jazz guitarist Chris Standring for the live album recording in concert at Cadogan Hall, London (2016).

Jazz Music in the UK

Although we now have many recordings of jazz music that can be traced back for over some 100 years, jazz is at its most innovative and exciting when heard live. Here in the UK we have many amazing and talented jazz musicians who continue creating accessible and original jazz. Jazz clubs and venues are peppered throughout our cities of the UK, Europe and internationally. With a little research and experimentation, it is possible to see and hear top class jazz every day of the week. Discovering jazz music as a jazz dancer, being involved musically, can make for an inspiring experience and provides a live experience to the aural development for the jazz dancer.

Jazz Artists

- Kamasi Washington
- Django Bates
- Empirical
- Sons of Kemet
- Liane Carroll
- Jamie Cullum
- Graham Harvey
- Gwyneth Herbert
- Gwilym Simcock
- Gareth Williams
- Jason Rebello
- John Taylor
- Dave Holland
- Arnie Somogergy
- Steve Watts
- Julian Arguelles
- Evan Parker
- Iain Ballamy
- Denys Baptisite
- Yolanda Brown
- Nathaniel Facey
- Nigel Hitchcock
- Soweto Kinch
- Toni Kofi
- Dave O'Higgins
- Courtney Pine
- Julian Siegel
- Martin Speake
- Stan Sulzman
- Jason Yarde
- Martin France
- Barb Jungr
- Juliet Kelly
- Anita Wardel
- Mark Lockheart
- Brad Mehldau
- Gary Crosby
- Julian Joseph
- Ray Gelato
- Shane Forbes
- Clark Tracey
- Mark Mondesir
- Jazz Warriors
- John Etheridge
- Judi Jackson
- Billy Jenkins
- Zara McFarlane
- Jim Mullen
- Chris Standring
- Martin Taylor
- Guy Barker
- Gerard Presencer
- Byron Wallen
- Loose Tubes
- Jacqui Dankworth
- Julie Dexter
- Claire Martin
- China Moses
- Tomorrow's Warriors
- Tina May
- Clare Teal
- Cleveland Watkiss
- Jay Phelps
- Rueben James
- Shabaka Hutchings
- Nubya Garcia
- Kit Downes

DANCE STUDIOS, PERFORMING ARTS ORGANIZATIONS AND JAZZ SERVICES

London Located Dance Studios (UK)

Base Dance Studios
4 Tinworth Street, London SE11 5EJ

Dance Attic
368 North End Road, London SW6 1LY

Dance Works
16 Balderton Street, London W1K 6TN

Flow Dance London
Unit 3 Kennington Business Park, Canterbury Court, London SW9 6DE

Pineapple Dance Studios
7 Langley Street, London WC2H

Siobhan Davies Studios
85 St Georges Rd, London SE1 6ER
Studio 68
68 Ewer Street, London SE1 0NR

Performing Arts Colleges (UK)

Birds College
Alma Road Sidcup, Kent DA14 4ED
The British School for Performing Arts and Technology
60 The Crescent, Croydon CR0 2HN
Italia Conti Academy of Theatre Arts
23 Goswell Rd, London EC1M 7AJ
Laine Theatre Arts
East St, Epsom, Surrey KT17 1HH
Liverpool Institute for Performing Arts
Mount Street, Liverpool L1 9HF
London Studio Centre
5 Nether St, London N12 0GA
Millennium Performing Arts
29 Thomas St, Woolwich, London SE18 6H
Mountview Academy of the Arts
120 Peckham Hill Street, London SE15 5JT
Performers College
Southend Road, Corringham, Essex SS17 8JS
Sylvia Young Theatre School
1 Nutford Place, London W1H 5YZ
The Place
17 Duke's Road, London WC1H 9PY
Trinity Laban Conservatoire of Music and Dance
King Charles Court, London SE10 9JF
Urdang Academy
The Old Finsbury Town Hall, Rosebery Avenue, London EC1R 4RP
Wilkes Academy
1 Westmead Industrial Estate, Westmead Drive, Swindon SN5 7YT

Universities That Offer Dance Programmes (UK)

Chichester College
Westgate Fields, Chichester, West Sussex PO19 1SB
Middlesex University
The Burroughs, Hendon, London NW4 4BT
University of Roehampton London
Grove House, Roehampton Lane, London SW15 5PJ
University of Surrey
Guildford, Surrey GU2 7XH

United States

Ailey Extension
405 W 55th St, New York, NY 10019
Broadway Dance Center
322 W 45th St, New York, NY 10036
Debbie Allen Dance Academy
3791 Santa Rosalia Drive, Los Angeles, CA 90008
Duke Ellington School of the Arts
3500 R Street NW, Washington, DC 20007
Edge Performing Arts Center
6300 Romaine St #100, Los Angeles, CA 90038
Cumbe: Center for African and Diaspora Dance
1368 Fulton St, Brooklyn, NY 11216
Giordano Dance Chicago
1754 N Clark Street, Chicago, IL 60614
Katherine Dunham Centers for the Arts and Humanities
532 Katherine Dunham Place, East Saint Louis, IL 62201
Liberated Movement
380 Broadway 5th Floor, New York, NY 10013
Mark Morris Dance Center
3 Lafayette Ave, Brooklyn, NY 11217
Peridance Capezio Center
126 E 13th St, New York, NY 10003
Steps on Broadway
2121 Broadway, New York, NY 10023

Europe

Institute of the Arts Barcelona
C/ Ramon Dalmases 18, 08870 Sitges, Spain
Rick Odums – Centre International de Danse de Jazz
54 Rue de Clichy, 75009 Paris, France

Studio Harmonic
5 Passage des Taillandiers, 75011 Paris, France
Centre De Danse Du Marais
41 Rue Du Temple, 75004 Paris, France
Le Centre Des Arts Vivants
4 Rue Bréguet, 75011 Paris, France
Oslo National Academy of the Arts
Postboks 6853, St. Olavs plass 0130 Oslo, Norway

INTERNATIONAL JAZZ DANCE CONVENTIONS

Congresso de Jazz Dance
Rua das Primaveras, 210
www.congressodejazzdance.com.br
Indaiatuba|São Paulo|Brasil
Contact: Marcela Benvegnu and Erika Novachi
Giordano – Jazz Dance World Congress
1754 N Clark Street, Chicago, IL 60614
www.giordanodance.org
The International Association of Blacks in Dance, Inc.
8730 Georgia Avenue, Suite 606, Silver Spring, MD 20910, USA
www.iabdassociation.org

USEFUL WEBSITES AND DANCE PERIODICALS

Jazz Dance Direct
Created by Melanie George
Directory of International jazz dance and theatre companies
www.jazzdancedirect.com
One Dance UK – The UK Body for Dance
Ensign House, Battersea Reach, Juniper Drive, London SW18 1TA
www.onedanceuk.org
Dance of the African Diaspora at One Dance UK
Ensign House, Battersea Reach, Juniper Drive, London SW18 1TA
www.onedanceuk.org
Dancing Times Magazine (UK)
www.dancing-times.co.uk
Dance Europe (Europe)
www.danceeurope.net
Dance International (Canada)
http://danceinternational.org
Dance Mogul Magazine (USA)
www.dancemogul.com
Danser – Le Magazine de la Danse (France)
www.dansermag.com
Jazz Wise Music Magazine (UK)
www.jazzwisemagazine.com

The BOP company of musicians and dancers, *Miles Ahead Tour* (2013). BRENDON HANSFORD

ACKNOWLEDGEMENTS

We would like to acknowledge all BOP company performers, past and present (1996–2019) and all creatives' friends that have contributed so much to BOP over the last twenty-three years. An enormous thank you to all our dancers who feature in many of the photographs and to all the photographers who have gifted their work and allowed us to share their amazing images throughout the book. BOP Jazz love and thank you all.

Andrew Denton
Carly Fisher
Carrie Willis
Charlotte Tooth
David Olton
Diana Girbau
Elizabeth Holmes
Emily Kate Pettite
Emmanuella Idris
Gede Foster
Illaria Bellini
Jesus Santana Ramos
Joseph Hunt
Karen Walker
Katie Willy
Kerri de Aguiar
Kimberlee Collicutt
Leila Moniz
Leon Hazlewood
Lucia Cardona
Maria Quero Sanchez
Marina Climent Casas
Marité Querel
Marta Glowacka-Escote
Martina Farkasova
Matevz Cesen
Melvin LeBlanc
Nadia Strahan
Nicola McDonald
Patrice Moniz
Paul Bailey
Penny Ashcroft
Remy Martyn
Samantha Tan
Sarah Dos Santos
Tina Omotosho
Valentina Dolci

Photographers' Websites

Annalisa Banello Photography
www.annalisabanello.com
Bafana Solomon Matea Photography
www.mateaphotography.co.uk
Brendan Hansford http://brendonhansford.com
Brian Appiah Obeng
https://brokenjumps.carbonmade.com
Hugo Glendinning
www.hugoglendinning.com
Maya de Almeida Araujo
www.mayaalmeida.com
Nikita Alba Photography
www.nikitaalba.com
Simon Richardson
http://simonrichardson.org

OPPOSITE: **Dollie Henry performing *Lover Man* from the BOP Jazz Theatre production *Dizzy Heights***

SOURCE ACKNOWLEDGEMENTS

Chapter 1

P. 21 *The Story of American Vernacular Dance*, 2nd rev. edn written by Marshall and Jean Stearns (DaCapo Press, 1994)

Chapter 2

P. 32 Savion Glover: www.brainyquote.com/quotes/savion_glover_759047

P. 32 Cholly Atkins: www.storemypic.com/album/cholly-atkins-quotes.rXA

P. 33 Donald O'Connor: www.azquotes.com/author/10955-Donald_O_Connor

P. 34 Bill Bojangles Robinson quotation: thinkexist.com/quotes/bill_bojangles_robinson/

P. 35 Harold Nicholas: https://quotefancy.com/quote/1575787/Harold-Nicholas

P. 36 Fred Astaire: www.azquotes.com/quote/521858/FredAstaire

P. 37 Sammy Davis Jr: www.azquotes.com/quote/73692/SammyDavisJr

P. 38 Gregory Hines: www.brainyquote.com/authors/gregory_hines

P. 39 Savion Glover: www.brainyquote.com/quotes/savion_glover_759086

Chapter 3

P. 47 Duke Ellington: www.brainyquote.com/quotes/duke_ellington_163735

P. 48 Dizzy Gillespie quotes: www.brainyquote.com/quotes/dizzy_gillespie_270324

P. 50 Miles Davis quotes: www.brainyquote.com/quotes/miles_davis_392896

Chapter 4

P. 60 Bob Fosse: www.azquotes.com/quote/532212

P. 60 Gene Kelly quotes: www.brainyquote.com/quotes/gene_kelly_449772

P. 65 Martha Graham – *The Evolution of Her Dance Theory and Training 1926–91*, 2nd rev. edn compiled by Marian Horosko (University Press of Florida, 2002)

P. 66 Katherine Dunham quotes: www.brainyquote.com/quotes/katherine_dunham_267100

P. 67 Pearl Primus: www.azquotes.com/quote/929470

P. 68 Alvin Ailey: www.azquotes.com/quote/1057577

P. 69 Donald McKayle from an interview with the *New York Times*. A version of this archive appears in print on 4 November 1973, on p.161 of the New York edition with the headline: With '*Raisin*,' *He Rises to the Top* by John Gruen: www.nytimes.com/1973/11/04/archives/with-raisin-he-rises-to-the-top-donald-mckayle-triumphs-as.html

P. 69 Dianne McIntyre defining the purpose and creative philosophy of her company Sounds in Motion from Ms McIntyre's website: www.diannemcintyre.com/index.htm

P. 71 Gus Giordano quote: www.gusgiordandance.com/jazzhistory

Chapter 6

P. 81 Shanna LaFleur: www.goodreads.com/quotes/6910647-it-takes-an-athlete-to-dance-but-an-artist-to

P. 83 Judith Jamison: www.dance-teacher.com/10-inspirational-quotes-from-famous-dancers-2508077590.html

Chapter 7

P. 106 African proverb: www.inspirationalstories.com/proverbs/t/west-african-on-dancing

Chapter 8

P. 137 Rhee Gold https://dancewherethemagicbegins.wordpress.com/2014/04/12/a-dance-teacher

Chapter 9

P. 145 Fabienne Fredrickson: www.goodreads.com/quotes/6491819-the-things-you-are-passionate-about-are-not-random-they

P. 150 Alvin Ailey: www.azquotes.com/quote/1057578

INDEX

Note: page numbers in **bold** refer to information contained in captions.